SYDNEY HARBOUR

SYDNEY HARBOUR

A GUIDE FROM NORTH HEAD TO SOUTH HEAD

BC and TF GORMAN

This book is dedicated to Maryann,
Amanda, Daniel and Christopher.

First published in Australia in 1999 by
New Holland Publishers (Australia) Pty Ltd
Sydney • Auckland • London • Cape Town

14 Aquatic Drive, Frenchs Forest NSW 2086, Australia
218 Lake Road, Northcote Auckland, New Zealand
24 Nutford Place, London W1H 6DQ, United Kingdom
80 McKenzie Street, Cape Town 8001, South Africa

All facilities, locations and amenities are described in this book as seen on the day or days when research was conducted during 1999. The authors make no claim that such facilities, locations or amenities will be as described at the time when this book is read or when any reader of this book visits such facilities, locations or amenities. The authors make no claims as to the safety of any beach or other facility, nor as to the presence of rescue equipment such as lifebelts.

National Library of Australia Cataloguing-in-Publication Data:
Gorman, Clem, 1942–
Sydney Harbour: a guide from North Head to South Head

Includes index.
ISBN 1 86436 429 7

1. Sydney Harbour (NSW) – Guidebooks. I. Gorman, Therese, 1944–. II. Title.

919.44104

Designer: Mark Thacker, Big Cat Design
Reproduction by: Times, Malaysia
Printer: Times, Malaysia

Acknowledgments

We would like to thank the following people who assisted us in researching this book:

Greg Benson, Gay Bilson, Susan Bridie, Barbara Coombes, Scott Crebbin, Lisa Darling, Kim Deluca, Bruce Dunn, Martin Ellis, Michael Freeland, Glen Marie Frost, Cmdr D.L. Garnock, Gerry Gleeson, John Hawkes, Wendy Hill, Lisa Holmes, Tim Jacobs, Elaine Kemp, Ian Kiernan, Beth Lawsen, Lucia and Sergio Lieto, Diane Massey, V.H.R. May, Nicole McConnell, Barry McGrath, Tony Moore, John Norton, Constable Jeff Olsen, Wendy Peacocke, Pauline Randall, Jacqui Ritchard, Rosalie Robinson, Megan Rushton, Bill Smith, Mike Stringer, Warwick Tiernan, Kylie Yates and the anglers of Sydney Harbour.

Without their ideas, information and enthusiasm this book would not have been possible.

Photographic Acknowledgments

All photographs by **Shaen Adey/NHIL** with the exception of the following:
Nick Rains/NHIL: front cover – main image, panel images B, C, F; back cover – panel images A, B; pp. 7, 8 (top), 9, 13, 47 (bottom), 51 (top), 53 (top), 94 (bottom), 133.
Anthony Johnson/NHIL: front cover – panel image D; pp. 10–11, 14 (top), 50, 54, 90–91, 93 (bottom).

Foreword

Sydney Harbour was nominated by Captain Arthur Philip over 200 years ago as the finest harbour in the world. It still has that status. I was fortunate to have been born on its shores and to grow up with it as my playground, and I have had a love affair with it spanning more than half a century. While taken with its great beauty, I have often fantasised as to how it must have looked in 1788.

It was my participation in the BOC Single Handed Around the World Race that reminded me that all was not well with this wonderful asset, and the race was the catalyst that led me to encourage a group of friends to organise the first Clean Up Sydney Harbour Day in 1989.

Through that process, we were able to remind people that such a wonderful asset belongs to all of us and that it is our responsibility, as individuals, to nurture and preserve it for one another, for our kids and for our kids' kids.

Now, with more than ten years of Clean Up activities, the harbour is clearly in the the ownership of the people, and it is getting cleaner every day. It was a great feeling to cruise the harbour's beaches in the first light of this year's Clean Up Australia Day and see so many of the beaches in an essentially pristine state. That would not have been the case ten years ago.

People have taken the lead, and encouraged a whole range of actions by governments and authoritities to match community action. There are now many more budgeted capital works planned or in progress that will improve further the quality of Sydney Harbour and other waterways.

Two examples of this include, firstly, the wealthy Sydney sailor who has funded the repair of Parsley Bay where he has lived all of his life, and secondly, the 60 million dollars in stormwater grants that we were able to convince the New South Wales Government to apply to stormwater management. A good proportion of those grants are being applied to Sydney Harbour.

I am pleased to support this book, primarily because it will help so many people, locals and visitors alike, to enjoy Sydney's wonderful harbour. Hopefully it will encourage all of these people through their considerate action to take a role in the health of what belongs to us all.

Tread lightly, and throw nothing in the Harbour or catchments—after all, a cigarette butt dropped in the street or on the beach may easily end up in the beautiful microcosm that is the rock pool that you wanted to show and share with someone.

In the same way, the action of turning over one rock, or the removal of one shell, one shellfish or one anemone might seem trivial. It is not. They are important, living parts of the magic, the mystery, the beauty of this, the finest Harbour in the world. Enjoy it and this book, and at the same time remember—the future is in our hands.

Ian Kiernan

Chairman and Founder of

Clean Up Australia

Clean Up the World

Contents

Preface

This book was written after we became aware that many people—including many Sydneysiders—do not really know Sydney Harbour, but would love to discover it. On their behalf we set out like intrepid modern-day explorers to find the harbour, to seek out its hidden details as well as its more majestic manifestations. We now take great pleasure in passing this information on to you.

From secret hideaway beaches, almost unchanged for centuries, to contemporary urban tourist developments less than a decade old, Sydney Harbour has just about everything a visitor could want. Both playground and workplace, the harbour is an old friend to those who know it well but, for thousands of visitors every year, it is an exciting new territory full of wonderful places to discover and explore.

We decided to trace the harbour anticlockwise from North Head to South Head, including entries for every bay, park or beach, only omitting the more inaccessible areas. While you may wish to browse through the book, dipping into a beach here or a park there, we suggest you go first to the 'Facilities at a Glance' section. Ordered alphabetically, this section offers listings of whatever amenity you may desire, whether it be boating, walking, fishing, enjoying a quiet beach or fine dining in a restaurant beside the water. Page references indicate where to find more information about a particular spot or facility and, for further details, relevant contact numbers are also provided.

With this book in hand you should be well-equipped to discover the many delights of marvellous Sydney Harbour.

B.C. and T.F. Gorman

Introduction

No city in the world offers a sight more breathtaking than the one that greets the visitor entering Sydney Harbour through the heads. Bush-covered hills, shining beaches, leafy suburbs crowding the harbour's edge, an expanse of glistening water alive with yachts, launches and ferries and, in the distance, the imposing city skyline.

The harbour is not only the jewel of Sydney, it is one of Australia's finest single features. Yet, many Sydneysiders are only vaguely aware of what their harbour has to offer. And the many interstate and overseas visitors to Sydney have never had a guide like this to help them discover and enjoy this magnificent place.

We set out to change all that. We have provided an inspirational guide to all that Sydney Harbour offers—from parks, beaches and fishing spots to playgrounds, boat-launch ramps and carparks; from kiosks and restaurants to Taronga Zoo and the Sydney Opera House. With text covering each harbourside spot accessible to the public, easy-to-read maps and the useful Facilities at a Glance listings, this book brings every part of the harbour to life for readers.

Not many harbours or shorelines allow you to park your car, have a swim and a shower and then dine haute cuisine beside the water all at the same spot. Yet, around Sydney Harbour there are many such places, including Nielsen Park, Clontarf Park, Balmoral, Rose Bay, Watsons Bay and Manly. Few if any other harbours offer such an exciting range of activities for children. Taronga Zoo, Oceanworld, the Australian National Maritime Museum and the Sydney Aquarium all add to Sydney Harbour's overwhelming appeal.

In the past, harbour access was sometimes difficult, but that has changed. Enlightened State and local governments have opened up new walks and new waterside parks and these have been followed by new marinas, new restaurants, new ferry services and new retail centres.

Spectacular developments like those in Darling Harbour, Pyrmont and Sydney Cove have brought the best of the harbour, and the best of our sophisticated lifestyles, together on the city's doorstep. And this has gone hand in hand with an immense improvement in the quality of the water in the harbour, brought about by a continuing State government policy of building new stormwater diversions, by tougher environmental safeguards and by the creation and expansion of the Sydney Harbour National Park.

Moreover, all this has been done without sacrificing the 'working harbour'. Cargo ships, cruise ships, tugs, pile-drivers, barges and commercial fishing boats ply the harbour night and day, adding colour and character to the scene. During the Year 2000 Olympics there will be an even greater buzz of activity, for the harbour will serve as an aquatic sports venue, with some areas temporarily taken over by Olympic authorities for events such as sailing.

Certainly, when Sydneysiders celebrate—whether it's the Bicentennial, Australia Day, New Year's Eve, the Ferrython, the Sydney Harbour Jazz Festival, the Dragon-Boat races or the Sydney–Hobart Yacht Race—it is at the harbour, the soul of Sydney, that they gather. Over these waters, fireworks crackle and sparkle; along these shores, good-natured crowds mingle and cheer.

This book will take you to every part of that soul. From little-known bush beaches, hidden away off side streets, to large precincts such as the Darling Harbour area, this book will be your guide and companion.

How to Use This Book

This book is structured to provide an easy-to-use yet comprehensive reference to every bay, park or beach accessible from land. This is not a book for the sailor looking for a secluded bay to anchor his boat; rather it is for both locals and visitors looking for a harbourside location in which to go for a walk, go fishing, enjoy some fine dining at one of the many restaurants, or a relaxed picnic on the grass.

Divided into seven sections covering the entire stretch of harbour between North Head and South Head, the book covers one location per page. Each entry includes a brief description of the site, while the accompanying key lists transport access and all available amenities. 'Top spot' indicates a particularly noteworthy location—these are also listed separately on page 6. One main map covering the entire harbour together with a map at the beginning of each section enable the reader to find their bearings quickly.

The last section is a detailed alphabetical list of facilities. If you're looking for a place to launch your boat, catch a ferry or have a great meal with splendid harbour views, this is where to start. A comprehensive index adds to the ease of reference.

So, pick up this book and begin exploring Sydney's spectacular harbour.

Sydney Harbour

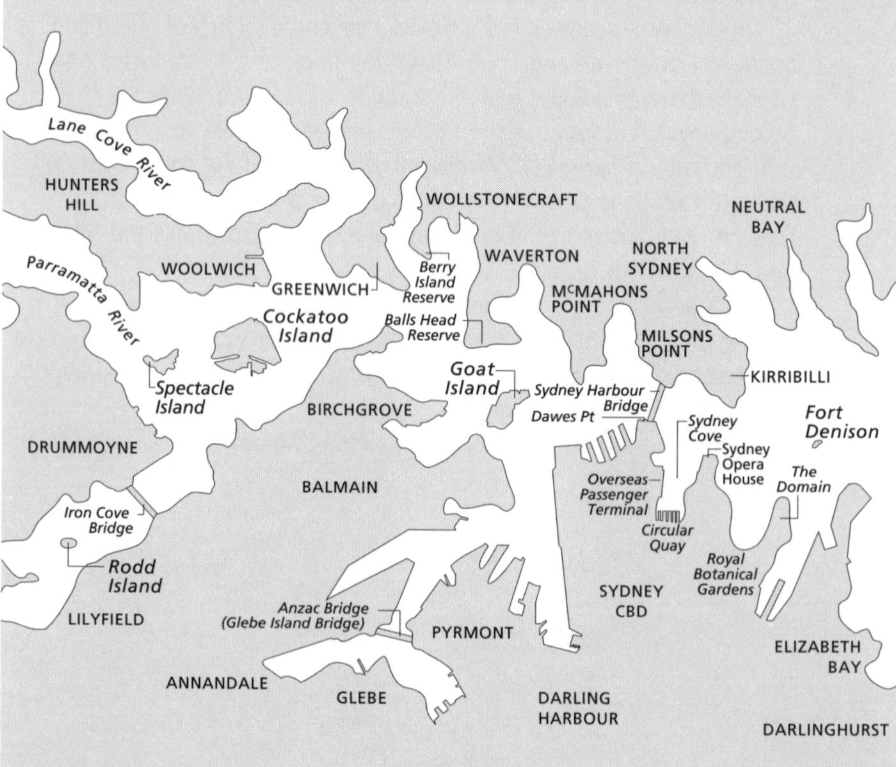

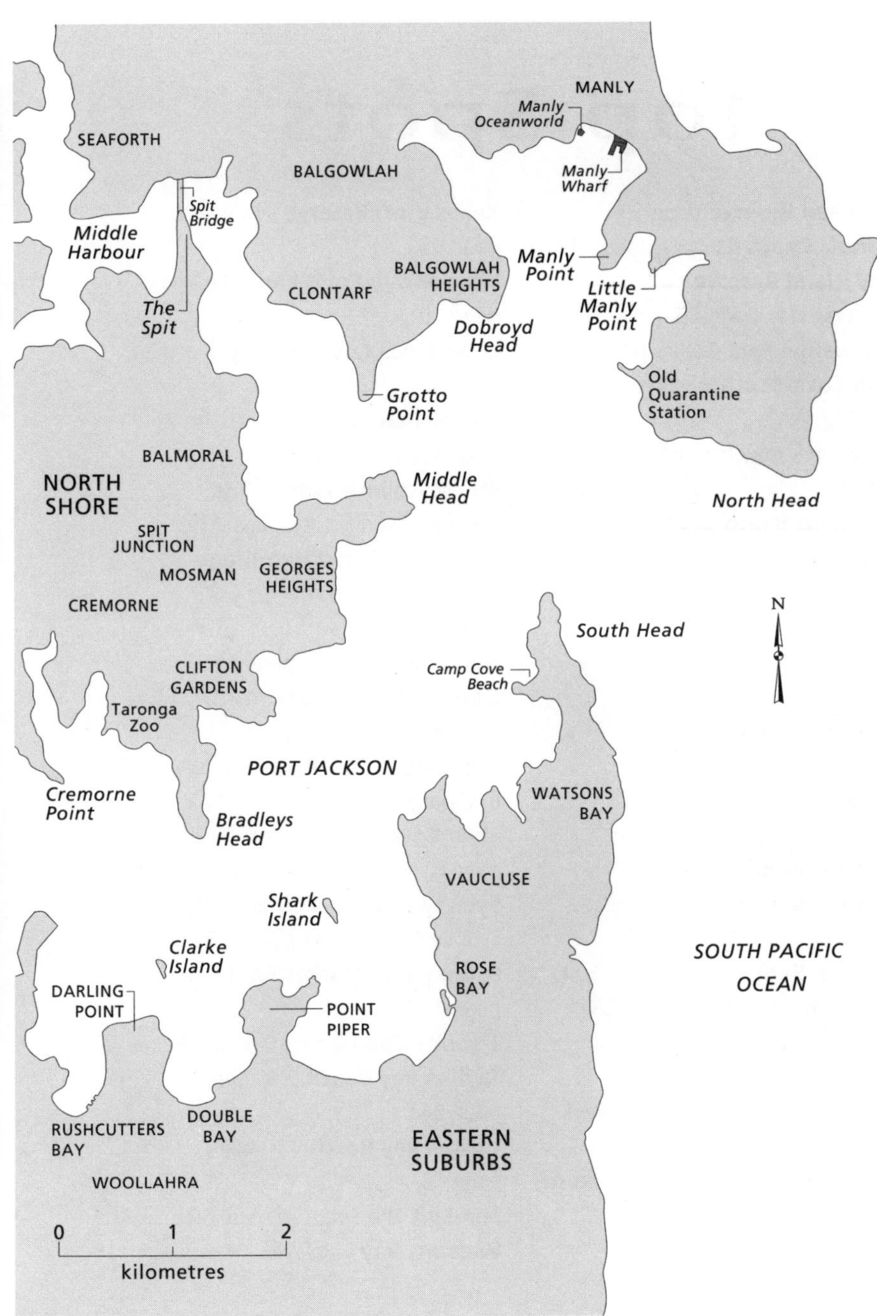
MANLY
Manly Oceanworld
SEAFORTH
BALGOWLAH
Manly Wharf
Spit Bridge
Middle Harbour
Manly Point
BALGOWLAH HEIGHTS
CLONTARF
Little Manly Point
The Spit
Dobroyd Head
Old Quarantine Station
Grotto Point
BALMORAL
NORTH SHORE
Middle Head
North Head
SPIT JUNCTION
MOSMAN
GEORGES HEIGHTS
CREMORNE
N
South Head
CLIFTON GARDENS
Camp Cove Beach
Taronga Zoo
PORT JACKSON
WATSONS BAY
Cremorne Point
Bradleys Head
VAUCLUSE
Shark Island
Clarke Island
SOUTH PACIFIC OCEAN
ROSE BAY
DARLING POINT
POINT PIPER
RUSHCUTTERS BAY
DOUBLE BAY
EASTERN SUBURBS
WOOLLAHRA
0
1
2
kilometres

Top Spots

While a busy traffic area for cars and boats, The Spit features sublime picnic spots.

Manly Wharf is a popular harbourside retreat.

The colonnade at Manly Pier Restaurant provides a pleasant walkway.

Manly's main thoroughfare, The Corso, straddles the peninsula between the ocean and the harbour.

North Head fronts a majestic vista of the harbour and distant cityscape.

Above: Clontarf marina and beach is a delightfully tranquil location.
Opposite at top: Dobroyd Head, in Sydney Harbour National Park, features in the Spit to Manly walk.
Opposite at bottom: The lighthouse on Grotto Point, Middle Harbour.

Manly has a superb location between the harbour and the sea.

Oceanworld on Manly Cove is a popular tourist destination.

North Head to Manly

From North Head to Manly is one of the most magnificent sections of the harbour. Here the huge ocean cliffs and coastal heathland scrub of rugged North Head, part of the Sydney Harbour National Park, change rapidly to small crescent-shaped harbour bush beaches. These, in turn, give way to the high-density streets of Manly, built on a sand spit just a few metres above sea level.

Once a holiday village 'seven miles from Sydney and a thousand miles from care', Manly today seems very close to the city. Speeding Jetcats now share the famous ferry route between Manly Wharf and Circular Quay, and the area is visited by huge numbers of people every year. Comparatively few, however, visit the wild bush headland; most head straight for the ocean beach.

While a morning visit to Manly is possible, exploration of the whole area requires a full day. If using public transport be prepared for long walks to the more beautiful parts. It is safe to promise, however, that no visitor to this spectacular section of the harbour will go away disappointed.

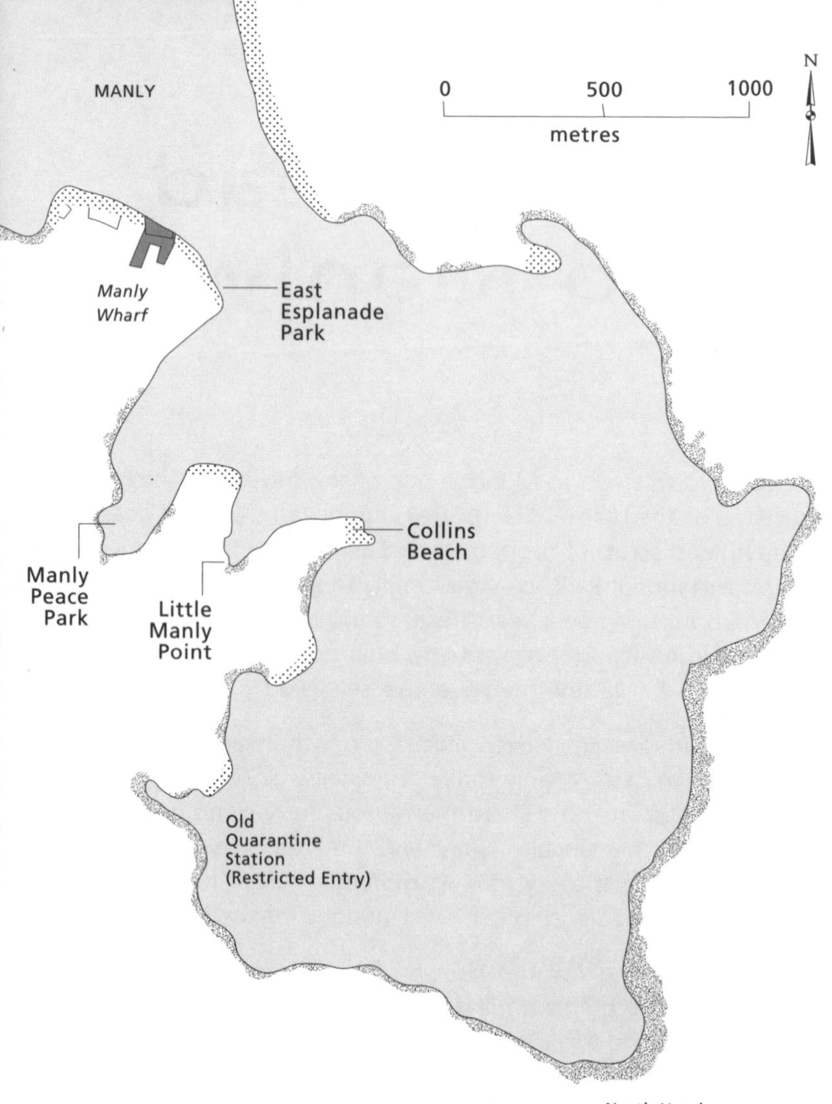
MANLY
0
500
1000
metres
N
Manly
Wharf
East
Esplanade
Park
Collins
Beach
Manly
Peace
Park
Little
Manly
Point
Old
Quarantine
Station
(Restricted Entry)
North Head

North Head, Manly

Top Spot

Much of North Head is part of Sydney Harbour National Park and, being quite elevated, the **views** are staggering. On one side, the vista extends up the harbour all the way to the city skyline. On the other, the views over the sheer cliffs and out to sea are equally breathtaking. While there is little provision for picnicking, this is a must-see area for a grand-scale picture of Sydney Harbour.

In recent years the National Parks and Wildlife Service has regenerated large areas of derelict bushland here and, despite numerous visitors, the area has a pristine naturalness about it. Care should be taken to stay on pathways to spare the vegetation.

There are gun emplacements from World War II and the 1850s to be seen, and North Head is also home to several **historical** naval buildings. The old Quarantine Station, now a conference centre (see Conference and Catering Venues, page 156) and historical site, offers interesting conducted tours, including ghost tours on summer evenings.

Fishing is prohibited at North Harbour Aquatic Reserve and access via the ladder, attached precariously to the cliff face, has been closed because it is too dangerous.

To get to this area by car, follow North Head Scenic Drive past Manly Hospital to the end of the road where there is plenty of ticketed parking and short walking tracks. The area is also accessible by **wheelchair** and **bike**, but bikes are not allowed on walking tracks. The gates are closed between 10 pm and 5 am.

Ferry: *to Manly Wharf.*
Bus: *from Manly Wharf to North Head, no. 135; to Manly Wharf, nos 131–2, 136, 139, 140, 141, 142, 143–4, 146, 151, 155, 156, 159, 169, 171, leaving a walk of more than three kilometres.*
Train: *none.*
Car: *access from North Head Scenic Drive, Manly.*
Water taxi: *none.*
Amenities: *bike access, fishing, parking, seating, views, walking, wheelchair access.*

Collins Beach, North Head, Manly

This pretty little stretch of sand is one of the few unspoilt **beaches** on the harbour. Like many others in Sydney Harbour National Park, it offers only limited amenities but its charm lies in being a delightful, unspoilt, bush-fringed hideaway. There are also lovely **views** over to South Head and the Eastern Suburbs.

For those who enjoy getting away from the urban rush but don't have the time to go farther afield, you can frolic here close to nature or just be—and let nature frolic all around you. This beach, which probably looks much as it did when first seen by British settlers, also offers a gory taste of history. Governor Phillip was speared here in 1792 while watching Aboriginal people feasting on whales.

Collins Beach can be reached by a **walk** through bush at the end of Stuart Street in Little Manly Cove, Manly. Although short, the track is a little rough in places and there is no bike or wheelchair access. The beach is also **accessible** by **boat** at high tide. While there is no public transport from Manly, the beach is less than two kilometres from Manly Wharf.

Ferry: *to Manly Wharf.*
Bus: *to Manly Wharf, nos.131–2, 136, 139, 140, 141, 142, 143–4, 146, 151, 155, 156, 159, 169, 171, leaving a walk of about a kilometre; from Manly Wharf to North Head, no. 135.*
Train: *none.*
Car: *access from Stuart Street, Manly.*
Water taxi: *none.*
Amenities: *beach, park, sailboard access, views, walking.*

Little Manly Point Park, Manly

Top Spot

Now one of the finest **parks** on the harbour, it is hard to believe this was once a gasworks, bits of which can still be seen. This is an excellent example of how to convert an industrial site on the harbour successfully into a beautiful environment for the entire community to enjoy. The terraced, open grasslands offer excellent **views** of the harbour.

A substantial, elevated park, Little Manly Point Park is perfect for **picnicking** or just taking the air. There are **barbecues**, **picnic tables**, **seating** and **shade**—everything you need to make open-air eating easy.

This is also an area where you can have all kinds of fun. A **beach** and a **boat ramp** are adjacent to the main park. **Sailboards** can be launched from here—but be careful not to sailboard into the prohibited area in the middle of Manly Cove.

There is **wheelchair** and **bike access** and plenty of nearby **parking**. People often **fish** here at the **jetty**.

Ferry: *to Manly Wharf.*
Bus: *to Manly Wharf, nos 131–2, 136, 139, 140, 141, 142, 143–4, 146, 151, 155, 156, 159, 169, 171, leaving a walk of around a kilometre.*
Train: *none.*
Car: *access from Stuart Street, Manly.*
Water taxi: *none.*
Amenities: *barbecues, beach, beach showers, bike access, boat ramp, jetty, kiosk, playground, park, parking, phones, picnic tables, sailboard access, seating, shade, toilets, views, wheelchair access.*

Manly Peace Park, Manly

While this tiny elevated **park** is of interest for its symbolism, it also has sensational **views** straight down the harbour. A grassed area the size of a large building block, with a few trees as well as a rocky area just above the water, it was established in 1986 to commemorate the International Year of Peace.

Wedged in between the prominent round apartment building on the end of Manly Point and a private hospital, the **views** down the harbour and across to North Head are impressive, but this park has virtually no amenities. However, if what you feel like doing is sitting on a **seat** in the sun looking at the harbour, this could be a peaceful place to do so.

The park can be **accessed** by **bike** and **wheelchair**.

Ferry: *to Manly Wharf.*
Bus: *to Manly Wharf, nos 131–2, 136, 139, 140, 141, 142, 143–4, 146, 151, 155, 156, 159, 169, 171, leaving a walk of a little over a kilometre.*
Train: *none.*
Car: *access from Addison Road, Manly.*
Water taxi: *none.*
Amenities: *bike access, seating, views, wheelchair access.*

Wildlife Around the Harbour

While the wallabies have long gone, many possums—ring-tailed and brush-tailed—can be found all around the harbour. A colony of bandicoots live in the Sydney Harbour National Park at North Head where night tours are run from the old Quarantine Station to see the nocturnal wildlife. Most exotic of all, perhaps, is the colony of fairy penguins living on inaccessible rocks around North Head, sometimes venturing into the harbour as far as Collins Beach and Little Manly. Snakes can also still be found around the harbour, especially red- and yellow-bellied black snakes.

East Esplanade Park, Manly

This curved sliver of a **park** follows the esplanade east from Manly Wharf. The pleasant **beach** is backed by lots of open grass and lovely old trees that provide plenty of **shade**.

Amenities abound, including **picnic tables**, a kids' **playground** and **toilets** in the park itself as well as a kiosk, a bar, restaurants and a public **phone** nearby. Adjacent clubs—the Manly 16ft Skiff Sailing Club and the Manly Yacht Club—welcome visitors.

Although much-used by the locals and by people waiting for their ferry to arrive, you can usually find somewhere to sit, enjoy the greenery and watch the people-parade. On weekends, however, the grassed area can be covered with sailing boats as contestants prepare for races. If you prefer participation to contemplation, you can always launch a **sailboard** from the beach—but make sure you avoid the prohibited area in the middle of Manly Cove.

Parking is restricted and is often difficult, but it is just a short **walk** from Manly Wharf, the terminus for numerous **buses**, the **ferry** and the **Jetcat**. There is also **bike** and **wheelchair** access and you can pull a **boat** close in to shore.

Ferry: *to Manly Wharf, right next door.*
Bus: *to Manly Wharf, nos 131–2, 136, 139, 140, 141, 142, 143–4, 146, 151, 155, 156, 159, 169, 171.*
Train: *none.*
Car: *access from East Esplanade, Manly.*
Water taxi: *to Manly Wharf.*
Amenities: *beach, beach shower, bike access, boat hire, limited parking, park, picnic tables, phone, playground, sailboard access, seats, shade, toilets, walking, wheelchair access.*

Manly Wharf, Manly

Built around the Manly terminus of the famous Manly Ferry, the wharf complex, partly constructed on poles over the water, juts into Manly Cove slicing the beach in two. The complex includes a shopping centre, **toilets**, a bar with excellent water **views**, several fine restaurants, including Armstrongs and Manly Cove Restaurant, some takeaway food outlets, a popular waffle and coffee bar, and a **jetty**.

Waiting for the ferry (or for a speedy Jetcat) provides the perfect opportunity for a spot of people-watching. Children romp in the **playground** or take a ride back in time on the ferris wheel. Enthusiasts fish from the jetty despite the signs prohibiting fishing. Last-minute shoppers shop, people meet friends and commuters take time out to listen to the lapping of the waves on the piles. It is possible to **hire a boat** or try **parasailing** from this wharf.

Ramps from the wharf make both the ferry and the Jetcat **wheelchair accessible**.

Ferry: *to Manly Wharf.*
Bus: *to Manly Wharf, nos 131–2, 136, 139, 140, 141, 142, 143–4, 146, 151, 155, 156, 159, 169, 171.*
Train: *none.*
Car: *access from East/West Esplanade.*
Water taxi: *to Manly Wharf.*
Amenities: *bike access, boat hire, jetty, parasailing, phones, playground, seating, shade, toilets, views, wheelchair access.*

The Manly Ferry

This service began in 1853 when Henry Gilbert chartered the wooden paddle steamer The Brothers *for occasional trips from Circular Quay to attract buyers to his newly subdivided land at Manly.*

Manly to The Spit

The stretch of harbour from Manly to The Spit can be explored a little at a time—beach by beach and park by park—but you might prefer to jump straight in and see it all in one day by undertaking the longest and one of the most spectacular of Sydney's harbour walks. From West Esplanade Park to The Spit this walk covers more than five kilometres, exploring every cove and cranny of this most varied section of the harbour (see Manly–The Spit in the Walks section, page 173).

The section includes numerous beaches, marvellous wild bushland, spectacular views and beautiful suburbs. Grassy strips and cosy beaches backed by houses along the water's edge near Manly lie in sharp contrast to the woolly heath-covered heights of Dobroyd Head, part of the Sydney Harbour National Park. From this elevated area magnificent views through the heads vie with city vistas up the harbour.

Among the bushier beaches, Castle Rock and Forty Baskets stand out, while toward The Spit, Clontarf Reserve, with its many amenities, is perhaps the best family picnic area. There are few places on this walk where refreshments may be purchased, so stock up before setting out. This walk is not for the unfit or the faint-hearted.

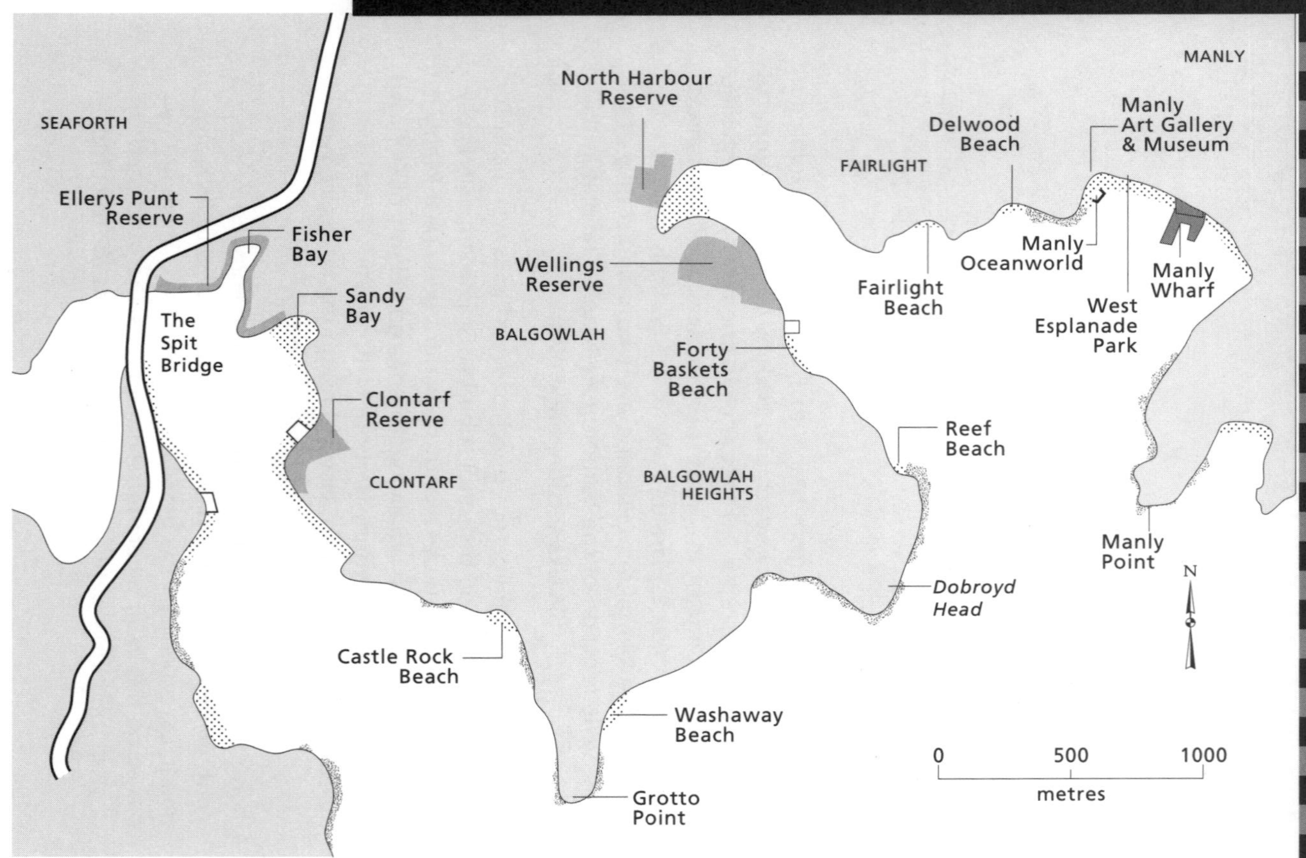
MANLY
SEAFORTH
North Harbour Reserve
Delwood Beach
Manly Art Gallery & Museum
FAIRLIGHT
Ellerys Punt Reserve
Fisher Bay
Wellings Reserve
Manly Oceanworld
Manly Wharf
Sandy Bay
Fairlight Beach
West Esplanade Park
The Spit Bridge
BALGOWLAH
Forty Baskets Beach
Clontarf Reserve
Reef Beach
CLONTARF
BALGOWLAH HEIGHTS
Manly Point
N
Dobroyd Head
Castle Rock Beach
Washaway Beach
0
500
1000
metres
Grotto Point

West Esplanade Park, Manly

Mature Norfolk Island Pines characterise this spacious, grassy **park** just west of Manly Wharf. With pleasant waterside **walking**, a small **beach**, part of which is enclosed for safe swimming, and many amenities, this spot is very suitable for people with children. The area features a modest **view** across Middle Harbour and more than a hint of culture in the form of the Manly Art Gallery and Museum—one of the best regional galleries in the Sydney area.

There are **picnic tables** (though no barbecues), **toilets**, plenty of **shade** and lots of **seating**. **Sailboards** can be launched from the beach, which usually appears clean but may be polluted by watercraft. Bikes must not be ridden in the park although they may be walked through it. Fishing is illegal.

The park is accessible by **wheelchair**, and although nearby **parking** is difficult and restricted to street only, there are several carparks in Manly within five minutes' walk, and the bus and ferry terminus at Manly Wharf is just a few metres away. Those visitors who are short of time may be able to walk, swim or picnic, and then catch a ferry back to the city, all within a few hours. This true urban park is used by high-rise apartment dwellers and visitors alike to cool off or just enjoy some space.

Ferry: *to Manly Wharf.*
Bus: *to Manly Wharf, nos 131–2, 136, 139, 140, 141, 142, 143–4, 146, 151, 155, 156, 159, 169, 171.*
Train: *none.*
Car: *access from West Esplanade, Manly.*
Water taxi: *to Manly Wharf.*
Amenities: *beach, beach showers, jetty, park, phone, picnic tables, pool, sailboard access, seating, shade, toilets, views, walking, wheelchair access.*

Oceanworld, Manly

This private marine park, close to Manly Wharf, is the only oceanarium in the world to be an accredited dive resort. This means not only can you watch divers feed sharks and other fish underwater but you, too, can dive with the big fish—if you are qualified. If you are not a qualified diver but the prospect of communing with underwater creatures seems irresistible, you're in luck—Oceanworld also runs a diving school.

For those who would rather stay out of the water, a large range of ocean creatures in a simulated natural habitat can be seen through glass—Oceanworld was the first aquarium in Australia to introduce, in 1987, the exciting concept of underwater tunnel viewing. Visitors can also enjoy the antics of performing fur seals.

Open every day, except Christmas Day, Oceanworld is a family funspot with reasonable prices and amenities including a kiosk, gift shop and **toilets**. Oceanworld also runs an education program for student groups.

There is **wheelchair access** to the facility. Parking is not easy on nearby streets, but there is a **parking station** at Manly. Even so, if you are coming from the city it might be easier to take the ferry. If you want to make a day of it you can picnic in the adjacent park, visit the **waterworks** next door, or eat at one of Manly's many restaurants.

Ferry: *to nearby Manly Wharf.*
Bus: *to Manly Wharf, nos 131–2, 136, 139, 140, 141, 142, 143–4, 146, 151, 155, 156, 159, 169, 171.*
Train: *none.*
Car: *access from West Esplanade, Manly*
Water taxi: *to Oceanworld's own jetty.*
Amenities: *toilets, wheelchair access.*

Delwood Beach, Manly

Giving a sense of Sydney as it was when the pace of life was slower, this cosy little **beach** is possibly one of the most relaxing spots on the harbour and is a popular spot for swimming. There are **rock pools** and pleasant **views** of the heads, and a small grassy area behind. This is a relatively uncrowded alternative to the busier, larger, better-known beaches nearby, such as Manly or Fairlight.

There is excellent full **shade** provided by trees, some **seating**, and the grassy area provides a pleasant, if slightly hilly, **picnic** spot. The beach can be visited by **boat**. People **fish** from the beach, mostly early in the morning or at dusk.

The grassy area has **wheelchair access** and is easily reached on foot. This is a beach well-used by locals, but it is also frequented by visitors who pass through on the **walking** path that stretches all the way to The Spit. Parking nearby is difficult, especially on weekends, but the beach is close enough to the Manly Wharf bus and ferry terminus to make even a brief visit worthwhile.

Ferry: *to Manly Wharf, several hundred metres away*
Bus: *to Manly Wharf, nos 131–2, 136, 139, 140, 141, 142, 143–4, 146, 151, 155, 156, 159, 169, 171.*
Train: *none.*
Car: *access from Commonwealth Avenue, Manly*
Water taxi: *to Manly Wharf.*
Amenities: *beach, fishing, park, pool, seating, shade, views, walking, wheelchair access.*

Fairlight Beach, Manly

Top Spot

This pretty, well-appointed **beach** lies not far west of Manly Wharf, to which it is linked by a **walking** path that continues all the way to The Spit (see Manly–The Spit in the Walks section, page 173). Although busier than Delwood next door, Fairlight is still easygoing, uncluttered and quiet with fine **views** of the heads from the higher ground.

The pleasant beach, tucked in between two tiny rocky headlands, offers good, safe **swimming**—there is even a tidal swimming **pool**—as well as lots of open grassy space with a little **shade**, some **seating**, **picnic tables**, excellent **change rooms** and **toilets** and a freshwater open-air **shower**. People often enjoy **fishing** from the edge of the tidal pool, using hand-held lines and the beach can be used to launch **sailboards**. Ideal for picnicking, swimming, sunbathing or just pottering about on the extensive rock platform at low tide, this is a lovely spot.

Both the beach and the grassy areas can be accessed by **wheelchair**. **Parking** is difficult to find on the nearby streets, therefore it may be easier to come here by **ferry** or **bus**. Despite being a little farther from Manly Wharf, this spot is still ideal for a quick visit.

Ferry: *to Manly Wharf, about a kilometre away.*
Bus: *to Manly Wharf, nos 131–2, 136, 139, 140, 141, 142, 143–4, 146, 151, 155, 156, 159, 169, 171.*
Train: *none.*
Car: *access from Margaret Street, Manly.*
Water taxi: *to Manly Wharf.*
Amenities: *beach, fishing, park, pool, sailboard access, seating, shade, shower, toilets, views, walking, wheelchair access.*

North Harbour Reserve, Balgowlah

Many years ago, a swamp was filled in to create this peaceful, flat, open, two-hectare **park**. Just a short walk from Fairlight Beach, the grassy, open and lightly treed reserve is rarely crowded—partly because of its substantial size—even though it is sometimes visited by large family groups for picnics. Although it does not have a beach—mud flats stretch from the harbour wall at low tide—it does have an out-of-the-way feeling that is precious in a big city.

The reserve offers everything you need for a barbecue or picnic, including **picnic tables**, **barbecues**, a kids' **playground**, **shade** under spreading trees, **seating** and, of course, **toilets**. People often **fish** over the stone harbour wall and there is plenty of opportunity for **walking** (you can follow the walking path in either direction (see Manly–The Spit in the Walks section, page 173), and a **phone** at a small corner shop nearby. There is even a **basketball hoop**!

The reserve has **bike** and **wheelchair access**. Parking may be difficult in the nearby streets but there is a small free **carpark** off Lower Beach Street. If you are looking for a peaceful haven not too far from public transport for a pleasant family picnic or a game of touch football or cricket, this place is for you.

Ferry: *none.*
Bus: *nos 132, 133 & E71.*
Train: *none.*
Car: *access from Burton, Lower Beach or Condamine streets, Balgowlah.*
Water taxi: *none.*
Amenities: *barbecues, basketball hoop, bike access, carpark, fishing, park, phone, picnic tables, playground, seating, shade, toilets, walking, wheelchair access.*

Wellings Reserve, Balgowlah

This rugged area of native bushland sloping down to North Harbour from Balgowlah Heights features large clusters of picturesque blue gums growing from cracks in rocks. As the reserve has a steep gradient and is mostly rock, this area is not really suitable for picnicking. It is, however, ideal for alternative activities such as **bushwalking** and **nature study**.

The tracks winding through the area are short, though sloping, and are suitable for children, elderly people who are reasonably fit, and most adults. You might also choose to follow the Manly–The Spit **walking** path in either direction (see Manly–The Spit in the Walks section, page 173).

This reserve shares a **parking** area, which can be muddy after heavy rain, with adjacent Forty Baskets Beach—a lovely beach well worth a visit.

Because this park is administered by the National Parks and Wildlife Service, dogs are strictly prohibited.

Ferry: *none.*
Bus: *nos 133, 171, 178 & L80.*
Train: *none.*
Car: *access from Gourley Street, Balgowlah.*
Water taxi: *none.*
Amenities: *bushwalking, nature study, park, parking.*

Forty Baskets Beach, Balgowlah Heights

Top Spot

This small but enjoyable bush **beach** gives the impression of being miles from any city and, in 1898, it was. In that year the fishermen of this area sent forty baskets of fish across to North Head Quarantine Station for troops camped there awaiting transport to the Boer War. Today, little areas of grassy **park** behind the beach are ideal for picnics and there is plenty of **shade** to be found under many large and magnificent eucalypts.

A **playground** is a pleasant surprise in such a seemingly bushy location. There are also **picnic tables** and free **barbecues** as well as **seating**, **toilets**, a **jetty**, some rescue floats and, perhaps most attractive of all, a substantial enclosed harbour **pool** for the kiddies. The area also offers pleasant **views** towards Manly.

Sailboards can be launched from the beach and, of course, there is plenty of **walking** to be had around here (see Manly–The Spit in the Walks section, page 173).

Forty Baskets can be reached by the Manly–The Spit walking track but a **carpark** off Gourley Street provides easier access, though there is still a bit of a walk to the beach and no **wheelchair access**. **Bikes**, however, can be ridden or wheeled in.

Ferry: *none.*
Bus: *none.*
Train: *none.*
Car: *access from Beatty Street, Balgowlah, carpark off Gourley Street.*
Water taxi: *none.*
Amenities: *barbecues, beach, bike access, carpark, jetty, park, picnic tables, playground, pool, sailboard access, seating, shade, toilets, views, walking.*

Dobroyd Head, Balgowlah Heights

Top Spot

This magnificent area of wilderness, one of the more spectacular parts of the Sydney Harbour National Park, contains a number of unspoilt **beaches** and still looks very much as it must have before 1788 when the only occupants were the local Aboriginal people.

The **views** from the top of the hill behind the headland—over almost the entire harbour east of the Sydney Harbour Bridge and well out to sea—are breathtaking. Standing on a rocky outcrop, you feel as though you could reach out and touch the water, or the distant suburbs and city. Nearby, evidence of past inhabitants can be found—a groove in the rock where Aborigines once sharpened their fishing knives. Some old fishing shacks near Reef Beach are still used (with permits).

Most users of this wild part of the Sydney Harbour National Park are walkers. Only reasonably fit people should attempt to **walk** in this area, particularly on very hot days, because of the rugged nature of the terrain, the lack of available drinking water and the relative lack of shade above the beaches (see Manly–The Spit in the Walks section, page 173).

At the top of the hill there is a large **carpark** (there is no public transport to the area), and an open grassy area where people fly kites and model planes.

Fishing is prohibited as the waters off Dobroyd Head lie in the North Harbour Aquatic Reserve.

Ferry: *none.*
Bus: *none.*
Train: *none.*
Car: *access from Duke of Edinburgh Parade, Balgowlah.*
Water taxi: *none.*
Amenities: barbecues, *beaches, bike access, bush, carpark, children's playground, park, picnic tables, seating, views, walking.*

Reef Beach, Balgowlah Heights

Clinging to the Manly side of rugged Dobroyd Head, little Reef Beach, with a hillside of coastal scrub rising behind it, feels very remote. One of the more unspoilt **beaches** of the harbour, this is a place to get away from it all—to swim, to sunbake, to forget the world.

Cruisers anchoring just offshore all along this stretch of harbour give the area an almost Mediterrannean ambience, quite a contrast to the Reef Beach of the Great Depression. During the 1930s a community of homeless, unemployed people camped here, living off the fish they caught. More recently, the beach was a haven for nude bathers until complaints from walkers on the Manly–The Spit walk led to a change in council policy.

Surprisingly, this comparatively remote beach has **toilets**. There is also **shade** from trees, and **sailboards** could be launched from here—though it would be hard work lugging the sailboard to this spot. It is only a short **walk** to spots with much better **views** of North Harbour than those available from the beach.

The beach can be reached via a track through the Sydney Harbour National Park from Beatty Street, Balgowlah Heights, or the Manly–The Spit track from Forty Baskets Beach. Both walks require a reasonable level of fitness. There is no wheelchair or bike access to the beach and no public transport.

Ferry: *none.*
Bus: *none.*
Train: *none.*
Car: *access from Beatty Street, Balgowlah Heights (but there is still a substantial walk down steep slopes through the national park).*
Water taxi: *none.*
Amenities: *beach, park, sailboard access, shade, toilets, views, walking.*

Washaway Beach, Clontarf

Nestling into the cliffs just north of Grotto Point in the Sydney Harbour National Park, Washaway is ringed by native bush. This pretty little curved beach offers **views** across the water and an almost pristine environment in which to **swim** or sunbake. Occasionally, burnt wood from fires lit on the beach can be a bit of an eyesore, but the feeling of being removed from the buzz of the nearby city makes it fade into insignificance. Although poorly signposted and a difficult walk, it is well worth the effort to get to this nude beach.

There is no public transport near Washaway Beach and the trek from the nearest road should be undertaken by reasonably experienced walkers only. Join the Manly–The Spit track off the end of Cutler Road and head toward The Spit. A rough track leads down from the main track to the rocks above the beach and then it is a bit of a scramble down worn sandstone shelves to the sand.

Ferry: *none.*
Bus: *none.*
Train: *none.*
Car: *access from Cutler Road, Balgowlah Heights, a few hundred metres away.*
Water taxi: *none.*
Amenities: *beach, swimming, views, walking.*

Castle Rock Beach, Clontarf

Top Spot

Part of the Sydney Harbour National Park, this lovely, isolated, bush **beach** attracts many visitors on luxury launches, as well as bushwalkers passing through. Ideal for **swimming** and sunbathing, the spot offers rewarding **views** toward Mosman. Spectacular cliffs behind the beach give the impression of a castle.

The beach is small but has a reputation for safety and there are rocks on either side suitable for sunbathing. Although there are no toilets or seating, there is some **shade** and **sailboards** can be launched from the beach, though it would be hard work carrying one in. If you don't mind carrying your picnic basket a fair way on foot, this is a perfect spot for a get-away-from-it-all family picnic on the rocks—though there is relatively little open space for playing cricket or touch football.

There is no public transport nearby—the nearest street has ample **parking**—and there is no wheelchair access.

Ferry: *none.*
Bus: *none.*
Train: *none.*
Car: *access from Ogilvy Road, Balgowlah.*
Water taxi: *none.*
Amenities: *beach, parking, sailboard access, shade, swimming, views, walking.*

Clontarf Reserve, Clontarf

Top Spot This grassy **park** on Middle Harbour near the Spit Bridge is an excellent spot for a family day out. Large and flat with lots of big old **shady** trees, a long clean **beach** and many amenities, this reserve is very popular on weekends so make sure you arrive early.

Plenty of **picnic tables** provide **seating** for large family groups, and there is no shortage of **barbecues**. Clontarf also has a kiddies' **playground**, a good restaurant (Clonny's) and an enclosed harbour pool. People fish from the beach or jetty and **sailboards** can be launched from here. The beach is often crowded with children on hot summer days.

This park earned a place in history when Henry James O'Farrell, a vehement Irish republican, shot and wounded the Duke of Edinburgh here in 1868. The only sound you will hear these days, however, is the laughter of children and the sizzling of barbies—a real community funspot.

The ample **carpark**—metered like so many North Shore harbourside carparks—rarely fills up, perhaps because this spot can be reached by **bus**, **bike** and on foot (the reserve lies along the Manly–The Spit walk, see Manly–The Spit in the Walks section, page 173). There is also **wheelchair access**.

Ferry: *none.*
Bus: *132, E 71.*
Train: *none.*
Car: *access from Holmes Ave, or Sandy Bay Road, Balgowlah.*
Water taxi: *to the small wharf at Clontarf.*
Amenities: *barbecues, beach, bike access, carpark, jetty, park, phone, picnic tables, playground, pool, sailboard access, seating, shade, toilets, walking, wheelchair access.*

Sandy Bay, Clontarf

Almost directly opposite the Spit Bridge, a small, grassy **park** curves around a sometimes surprising expanse of sandy **beach** which varies in size according to the tides.

Sailboards can be launched from here—the whole of Middle Harbour is waiting to be explored—and some people indulge in a spot of **fishing**.

While amenities are limited, the beach is very accessible. There is plenty of street **parking** as well as **bike**, **walking** and **wheelchair** access.

Sandy Bay seems to be used mainly by the locals with many visitors preferring the excellent facilities of Clontarf Reserve, just next door.

Ferry: *none.*
Bus: *to nearby Clontarf Beach, nos 132, E71.*
Train: *none.*
Car: *access via Sandy Bay Road, Clontarf.*
Water taxi: *none.*
Amenities: *beach, bike access, fishing, park, parking, sailboard access, walking, wheelchair access.*

Fisher Bay, Balgowlah

A substantial area of wild bush—including patches of subtropical **rainforest**, a rarity on the harbour—lines the tiny creek above Fisher Bay's small, scraggly **beach**.

This spot offers a little **shade** as well as **fishing** and **walking**—it is the last bay before The Spit on the Manly–The Spit walk (see Manly–The Spit in the Walks section, page 173). **Sailboards** could be launched from here to explore Middle Harbour.

This spot is not too far from public transport with many **buses** passing through The Spit, a short walk from Fisher Bay, on their way to Manly. Street **parking** is available on nearby Avona Crescent, Seaforth, but there is no bike or wheelchair access.

Ferry: *none.*
Bus: *to The Spit, nos 143, 144.*
Train: *none.*
Car: *access from Avona Crescent, Seaforth, and walk along the Manly Scenic Walkway.*
Water taxi: *none.*
Amenities: *beach, fishing, parking, sailboard access, shade, walking.*

Ellerys Punt Reserve, Clontarf

This tiny park next to the Spit Bridge on the northern shore of Middle Harbour is named after the man who operated the old punt across the harbour at this spot before the first Spit Bridge was built in 1905. A tram used to run between the punt and Manly.

Although there is no beach, this is a pleasant grassy place to park and have lunch in the shade of spreading trees while enjoying the **view** across the water. There are **picnic tables** as well **seats** and **shade** and wood **barbecues**. People often **fish** here.

This spot can be reached by **bike** (although not on the walkway) or by **walking** (see Manly–The Spit in the Walks section, page 173) or by **car** if you are driving south along Manly Road. **Buses** to Manly and Balgowlah run along Manly Road, immediately adjacent. Limited **parking** is available and there is **wheelchair access**.

Ferry: *none.*
Bus: *to Manly Road, no 178, The Spit, nos 143, 144.*
Train: *none.*
Car: *access from Manly Road.*
Water taxi: *none.*
Amenities: *barbecues, bike access, fishing, park, parking, picnic tables, seating, shade, views, walking, wheelchair access.*

The Spit

Top Spot

This place was once a simple spit of sand reaching halfway across what is now Middle Harbour. Today, Spit Bridge and Spit Road dominate the area, but in spite of the rushing traffic, the opening and closing of the bridge and the large carparks on either side of the road, The Spit's many amenities make it one of the top spots on Sydney Harbour.

Two well-appointed **parks** range along either side of Spit Road with small but enjoyable **beaches**, **fishing** spots, a **boat ramp** and places where **sailboards** can be launched. There is also a **playground** as well as **picnic tables**, wood **barbecues**, **toilets**, **phones** and plenty of **parking** (metered).

The Spit also boasts a string of quality **restaurants** along its eastern side, including the excellent bistro of the Middle Harbour 16ft Skiff Club. Here you can sit on the balcony, soothed by a gentle harbour breeze, and while away your time watching people **fishing** or working on boats—very restful. (See the Restaurants and Cafes section, page 167, for further details.)

The Spit is easy to get to as buses run right along Spit Road. The parks are also accessible by **bike**, on foot or by **wheelchair**.

Ferry: *none.*
Bus: *to Spit Road, no. 178.*
Train: *none.*
Car: *access from Spit Road, The Spit.*
Water taxi: *to marina wharves.*
Amenities: *barbecues, beaches, bike access, boat hire, boat ramp, carpark, fishing, jetty, parks, phones, picnic tables, playground, sailboard access, seats, shade, toilets, walking, wheelchair access.*

The Spit to Sydney Harbour Bridge

Many well-equipped parks and delightful beaches lie along this beautiful section of Sydney Harbour. They are typically larger, more open and have better amenities than other parks on the harbour.

Expanses of bushland from Georges Heights to Mosman are waiting to be explored. Taronga Zoo and the surrounding rugged bushland of Bradleys Head make for a very enjoyable family day out. The Sydney Harbour National Park at Middle Head is even more wild and offers vantage points with views right out to sea as well as sheltering several secluded bush beaches.

Of course, much of The Spit to Harbour Bridge section is comparatively tamed. A long parkland strip, great for walkers, skirts the built-up area of Cremorne Point. Balmoral Beach combines a comparatively large stretch of sand with clean water and rocky outcrops to make it perhaps the finest beach on the harbour. Neighbouring Chinamans Beach also deserves a mention for its unusually white sand.

This is a beautiful section of Sydney, offering a range of possible activities from fine dining to secluded bush bathing.

Rosherville Reserve
Chinamans Beach
Grotto Point
THE SPIT
BALMORAL
Edwards Beach
Cobblers Beach
Middle Head
Balmoral Beach
SPIT JUNCTION
MOSMAN
GEORGES HEIGHTS
Obelisk Beach
NEUTRAL BAY
CREMORNE
Reid Park
Harnett Park
Curraghbeena Park
Clifton Gardens Reserve
Kesterton Park
Neutral Bay Wharf
Anderson Park
Little Sirius Cove Reserve
N
Shell Cove Park
Milson Park
Taronga Zoo
Taylors Bay Beach
Careening Cove
Cremorne Point
Whiting Beach
KIRRIBILLI
Kurraba Point Reserve
Athol Bay
Bradfield Park
Mary Booth Park
0
500
1000
metres
MILSONS POINT
North Sydney Wharf
Sydney harbour bridge
Beulah Street Park
Robertsons Point
Beulah Street Wharf
Bradleys Head

Chinamans Beach, The Spit

Top Spot

This lovely deep, quiet **beach** is backed by Rosherville Reserve—a large and very pleasant **park**. The beach itself has some of the whitest sand you will ever see. Why this should be so is a mystery, since most harbour beaches tend to be closer to yellow. Rarely crowded, Chinamans offers fine **views** across Middle Harbour toward Clontarf.

Clusters of trees in the grassy reserve provide substantial **shade** and, for those who do not want to be reminded of the city, there is little evidence of surrounding buildings. This spot is very popular with families and there is **seating**, a **playground** and **toilets**, but no barbecues. Young people enjoy ball games in the open spaces of the reserve and there are pleasant **walks** to be had. As with so many of these spots, people often **fish** in the early morning or evening. Chinamans is also well-known as one of the better places on the harbour from which to **sailboard**.

Both beach and reserve are easily reached by **bike**, **wheelchair** or on foot. Buses are plentiful along nearby Spit Road, less than a kilometre away, down a steep hill, and one route runs along Parriwi Road just behind the Reserve. The **carpark** is large, both metered and free spaces.

Ferry: *none.*
Bus: *along Spit Road, nos 143 & 144; at Parriwi Road, nos 178 & 229.*
Train: *none.*
Car: *access from McLean Crescent, Spit Junction.*
Water taxi: *none.*
Amenities: *beach, bike access, carpark, fishing, park, playground, sailboard access, seating, shade, toilets, views, walking, wheelchair access.*

Balmoral Beach, Balmoral

Top Spot

One of the jewels of the harbour, lovely Balmoral—fringed by a narrow **park** behind a beach-long promenade—offers excellent **views** of Middle Harbour. As big as many ocean beaches, it is actually two sandy crescents—Balmoral Beach at the southern end and Edwards Beach at the northern end—separated by tiny Rocky Point Island.

Balmoral/Edwards boasts a childrens' **playground** as well as **picnic tables**, **toilets** and **phones**, but also a good **kiosk**, and several fine **restaurants** including the excellent Watermark and Bathers Pavilion restaurants. There are lots of **seats** in the **shade** of the big, old Moreton Bay fig trees, and a **rotunda** is used for concerts and for staging Balmoral's Shakespeare plays each summer.

A large enclosed harbour **pool** offers safe swimming, and rescue life-rings are provided along the beach. The beach is also a popular **sailboarding** area, and sailboards are available for hire. There are change sheds, a **boat ramp** and a **jetty** with **boat hire**, and people often **fish** from both the jetty and the beach.

A summer ferry from Circular Quay runs regularly on weekends only, connecting with other beaches, and buses run right to the beach. There is also plenty of **parking** (free and metered), and the beach can be accessed by **bike** or **wheelchair**.

Ferry: *(summer Saturdays and Sundays only) approximately hourly service, on a loop route from Circular Quay.*
Bus: *nos 233, 257, 238.*
Train: *none.*
Car: *access from The Esplanade, Balmoral.*
Water taxi: *to the ferry wharf.*
Amenities: *beach, bike access, boat hire, boat ramp, carpark, change rooms, fishing, jetty, kiosk, park, phone, picnic tables, playground, pool, rotunda, sailboard access and hire, seating, shade, toilets, views, walking, wheelchair access.*

Cobblers Beach, Middle Head, Georges Heights

Top Spot This pretty bush **beach** is tucked into a small cove on the northern side of Middle Head—a densely forested part of the Sydney Harbour National Park.

The beach itself has no facilities (there is a **toilet** block at the baseball field above the beach, adjacent to the naval base) and it has to be stressed that the climb down is difficult and strenuous. This is, however, one of the loveliest unspoilt beaches on the harbour—a truly exquisite spot.

Cobblers' isolation has allowed it to be used as one of Sydney Harbour's few nude beaches, though it is not zoned as such. It is frequented by the gay community, mostly couples, as well as heterosexual people, singles or couples, all enjoying its relaxed atmosphere and hassle-free character. People don't fish much here, but those interested in **history** might like to discover more about the old Army tunnels from World War II criss-crossing the area.

Access to Cobblers is by foot only, down a short steep track from the northern side of the baseball field off Middle Head Road.

Ferry: *none.*
Bus: *none.*
Train: *none.*
Car: *access from Middle Head Road, Mosman.*
Water taxi: *none.*
Amenities: *beach, carpark, park, shade, toilets, walking (steep).*

Obelisk Beach, Middle Head, Georges Heights

Top Spot Obelisk Beach, on the southern side of the Middle Head peninsula, is so named because of the old obelisk that stands beside it. Small and clean, this lovely bush-fringed beach has fabulous **views** across the harbour to South Head.

Isolated Obelisk, like Cobblers, although not zoned as such, is used as a nude beach, primarily by the gay and lesbian community and, as people heading down to the beach from the free **carpark** above will assure you, anyone who enjoys the relaxed atmosphere is welcome.

The beach itself has no facilities, although both Cobblers and Obelisk are served by a **toilet** block beside the baseball field at the top of the peninsula, adjacent to the naval base.

Ferry: *none.*
Bus: *none.*
Train: *none.*
Car: *access from Middle Head Road, Mosman.*
Water taxi: *none.*
Amenities: *beach, carpark, sailboard access (long walk), shade, toilets, views.*

Middle Head, with HMAS *Penguin* and popular Balmoral Beach in the foreground.

Sailboarding is only one of many sports that can be enjoyed on Sydney Harbour.

Yachts bob on their moorings at Middle Harbour Yacht Club, The Spit.

Catalina Yachts

Taronga Park Zoo features a spectacular Sydney Harbour and city backdrop.

Sydney Opera House and Sydney Harbour Bridge.

The pure, white sand of Chinamans Beach, Middle Harbour.

The wharf at Clifton Gardens provides a safe swimming haven.

Admiralty House, Kirribilli, the Sydney residence of the Governor General.

An aerial view of Kirribilli and Sydney Harbour.

Many parts of the harbour are easily accessible by ferry.

Sydney Harbour is an exciting venue for the annual Australia Day celebrations.

By night, Sydney Harbour takes on a different character altogether.

Clifton Gardens

Top Spot

An expansive grassy reserve, most of which is part of Sydney Harbour National Park, extends back toward Mosman from a lovely sheltered **beach**. The area offers many amenities, but most valuable, perhaps, is the sense of space that this flat, open **park** affords—a highly desirable quality in a fairly densely populated area.

The atmosphere is relaxed and happy with large family groups often gathering under the **shade** of the huge Moreton Bay figs to enjoy a picnic. **Picnic tables**, toilets and seating contribute to the comfort of an afternoon in the fresh air. Kids run freely in the large open areas or fool around the **basketball hoop** or the **playground**; adults often throw frisbees or play around with a bat and ball.

Half the beach is enclosed by a large harbour **pool** which is generally clean (an adjacent naval station may mean the water is a little oily at times). **Rescue** life-rings are provided and there is also a **phone**.The beach can be used to launch **sailboards** and some people **fish** from the jetty.

A large **carpark** (metered) is located off Morella Road, but the area can also be accessed by **bus**, **bike** or a **water taxi** to the **jetty**. The park is **accessible** by **wheelchair**.

Ferry: *none.*
Bus: *no. 228.*
Train: *none.*
Car: *access from Kardinia Road.*
Water taxi: *to Clifton Gardens Wharf.*
Amenities: *beach, bike access, carpark, fishing, jetty, park, phone, picnic tables, playground, pool, sailboard access, seating, shade, sport, toilets, walking, wheelchair access.*

Taylors Bay Beach, Mosman

Top Spot This secluded smidgin of sand is typical of the marvellously unspoilt, wild beaches that may be found, with a little searching, around Sydney Harbour. With not much in the way of views and no amenities at all, it is nevertheless a tiny paradise—a bush-fringed **beach** where you can strip off the cares of city life, and a lot of visitors strip off more than that.

There are some nice **picnic** spots and plenty of **shade** though there are no open grassy areas. Just above the beach there is an excellent **walk** that runs all the way from Clifton Gardens, right around Bradleys Head to Whiting Beach, and then all the way to Little Sirius Cove.

The beach is reached via a long, difficult climb down a track that begins opposite the main entrance to Taronga Zoo or a shorter but still strenuous climb down from Iluka Avenue, Mosman. Whichever way you come, it is a fair walk from the nearest street parking or public transport. Make the effort, carry the picnic hamper, and just relax.

Ferry: *to Taronga Zoo Wharf.*
Bus: *to Taronga Zoo, less than a kilometre away, no. 247.*
Train: *none.*
Car: *access from Iluka Road, Clifton Gardens, 200 metres away.*
Water taxi: *none.*
Amenities: *beach, picnic, shade, walking.*

Bradleys Head, Mosman

This large bushy headland extends south from Taronga Zoo, offering superb **views** from the Zoo wharf or the grassy areas above it of the Eastern Suburbs, the busy harbour itself and the city towers glittering across the water.

While there is no beach, some small grassy areas have been carved out of the bush to make ideal **picnic** spots. There is also a modest **carpark**, a **toilet** block and lots of **seating**, including a **mini amphitheatre**, and **shade**. People **fish** from an old stone **jetty**.

Now a part of the Sydney Harbour National Park, the area was once considered critical to the defence of the harbour—remnants of an 1854 fort built into the side of the hill can be found just below the carpark. There is also a light beacon built in 1905 and the mast of HMAS *Sydney*—erected here in memory of the 645 sailors who died when the ship was sunk in World War II in the Indian Ocean.

The **park** can be reached by **bike** or on foot via the **walk** that stretches from Clifton Gardens to Little Sirius Cove. There is **wheelchair access** to much of the area.

Ferry: *to nearby Taronga Zoo Wharf.*
Bus: *to Taronga Zoo, no. 247.*
Train: *none.*
Car: *access from Bradleys Head Road, Mosman.*
Water taxi: *to Taronga Zoo Wharf.*
Amenities: *bike access, carpark, fishing, jetty, mini amphitheatre, park, picnicking, seating, shade, toilets, views, walking, wheelchair access.*

Taronga Zoo, Mosman

Top Spot Taronga Zoo's superb location on the side of the hill above Athol Bay gives rise to spectacular views over the harbour toward the city. These are especially dramatic at night (Taronga runs regular nocturnal tours) when the glowing city spreads out before you and the lights of passing ships wink in the dark.

Within the zoo itself there is plenty of **seating** and **shade** and, aside from the pleasure of communing with the animals, it is a pleasant area for **walking** or **picnicking**. There are cafes, kiosks and restaurants within the zoo walls, as well as souvenir shops, **phones** and the Conference and Catering Centre (see Conference Venues, p. 157), with stunning views across the harbour to the lights and heights of the city. The zoo offers a range of guided tours and is open every day of the year.

Taronga provides a more than ample **carpark** (paid), is **wheelchair accessible** and can also be reached by bus and ferry. A thrilling aerial cable car carries more adventurous visitors from the ferry to the top gate.

Ferry: *to Taronga Zoo Wharf.*
Bus: *to the main gate of Taronga Zoo, no. 247.*
Train: *none.*
Car: *access from Bradleys Head Road, Mosman.*
Water taxi: *to Taronga Zoo Wharf in Athol Bay.*
Amenities: *carpark, jetty, park, phone, picnicking, playground, seating, shade, views, walking, wheelchair access.*

Whiting Beach, Mosman

Thank God for the unspoilt beaches of Sydney Harbour! Beaches like Whiting are precious, bringing us back in touch with nature and showing us wild places within a stone's throw of urban hustle.

There are no amenities at all at Whiting Beach, just a curve of sand, clear water and lots of bush behind—a lovely place for a quiet day's **fishing** or **swimming**. The only negative is the lantana which, together with other weeds, is slowly choking the native bushland out of existence. As at other beaches within the Sydney Harbour National Park, volunteers directed by national parks staff are fighting the encroachment and it is not unusual to come across whole areas of denuded bushland where lantana and other weeds have been ripped out.

To reach Whiting, **walk** east from Little Sirius Cove or west from Taronga Zoo Wharf—less than a kilometre in either direction. The walk through dense bush is pleasant, with occasional tantalising glimpses of the water, and not too strenuous for a person in reasonable health. Here and there, a smaller path branches off to a lookout over the harbour.

Ferry: *to Taronga Zoo Wharf, about a kilometre away.*
Bus: *none.*
Train: *none.*
Car: *access from Athol Wharf Road.*
Water taxi: *to Taronga Zoo Wharf, about a kilometre away.*
Amenities: *beach, fishing, park, swimming, walking.*

Little Sirius Cove Reserve, Mosman

Top Spot This grassy, tree-filled park, with magnificent views across to Robertsons Point, joins the Sydney Harbour National Park halfway down Little Sirius Cove toward Whiting Beach. Flat in parts, hilly in parts, with lots of lovely **picnicking** spots and a crescent of beach at the head of the bay, this area is much enjoyed by family groups and fully deserves to be one of Sydney Harbour's top spots.

The reasonably large **beach** is very sheltered, which may be why it is a favourite spot for families, particularly those with small children. A smaller stretch of sand, tucked away in the bush, lies just east of the main beach. The reserve behind the beach has enough open space to accommodate ball games and frisbee throwing while also providing plenty of **shade**. There is also a kiddies' **playground**, **seating** and a **toilet** block. **Fishing** is a popular pastime in the area and **sailboards** can be launched from the beach. If that isn't enough to keep you occupied, there is plenty of **walking** to be had, both within the park and east toward Taronga Zoo and Bradleys Head.

A large free **carpark** lies off Sirius Cove Road, and the bus and ferry are a few hundred metres away at Musgrave Street Wharf. There is **bike** and **wheelchair access**.

Ferry: *to Musgrave Street Wharf, about 1 km away.*
Bus: *to Musgrave Street Wharf, nos 236 & 233.*
Train: *none.*
Car: *access from Sirius Cove Road, Mosman.*
Water taxi: *to Musgrave Street Wharf.*
Amenities: *beach, bike access, carpark, park, picnicking, playground, sailboard access, seating, shade, toilets, views, walking, wheelchair access.*

Curraghbeena Park, Mosman

Curraghbeena Park, on the western foreshore of Little Sirius Cove, is split in two by Curraghbeena Road. The eastern or cove section of the **park** is steep, heavily forested and inaccessible from the roadway. The western section, sandwiched between Curraghbeena Road and Raglan Street, is quite different. Open grassy areas offer some **shade**, **seating** and **views** of the Sydney skyline. There is a childrens' **playground** and a modest amount of street **parking**.

This is a pleasant enough place to take the air on a summer's evening but there is nothing special here to attract a visitor or tourist.

Ferry: *to Musgrave Street Wharf, a short walk away.*
Bus: *to Musgrave Street Wharf, nos 236 & 233.*
Train: *none.*
Car: *access from Curraghbeena Road, Mosman.*
Water taxi: *to Musgrave Street Wharf, a short walk away.*
Amenities: *park, parking, playground, seating, shade, views.*

The Artists Camp at Little Sirius Cove

Between 1891 and 1896 artists Tom Roberts and Arthur Streeton lived for part of each year at an Artists Camp they established at Mosman Bay—probably around the area known today as Little Sirius Cove. Their motivation was partly poverty, especially in Roberts' case, but it was here that they were inspired to paint some of their most famous landscapes. Roberts, known to posterity as the father of Australian landscape, had very little success in his lifetime and was always poor. Streeton was more successful financially but liked to get away from it all at Mosman Bay, which was not settled in those days. Other artists spent varying amounts of time at the camp.

Harnett Park and surrounds, Cremorne and Mosman

Top Spot Harnett Park, a wonderful steeply sloping waterside reserve, threaded by a **walking** track, stretches in a narrow bushy band along the eastern side of Cremorne Point to link up with lovely Cremorne Reserve on the point. At its northern end, Harnett opens out onto Reid Park—a wide, grassy area, fringed by native bushland and ideal for **picnics**—a combination of wild bushland and well-appointed parkland.

Reid Park features a kiddies' **playground**, **picnic tables**, **toilets** and a **phone**. There is also plenty of seating and, if you get sick of relaxing in the **shade**, **sailboards** can be launched from here and fishing is popular but illegal from the ferry wharves. Reid Park is open enough for kicking a football and there are even permanent pitches for cricket. Or take a walk on the (semi) wild side and follow the track around Cremorne Point to Shell Cove beach, enjoying lovely **views** across the harbour.

Of course, you mustn't leave the area without visiting the Mosman Rowers Club—a Sydney institution (see the Clubs section, page 155). The club offers waterside al fresco dining or a more formal setting and a bar.

A large free **carpark** is located off Harnett Avenue, and the area can be reached by ferry, **bike** or on foot. Reid Park is **wheelchair accessible**.

Ferry: *to Old Cremorne Wharf, near the Mosman Rowers Club.*
Bus: *to Milson Road, Cremorne Point, nos 225 & 226.*
Train: *none.*
Car: *access from Harnett Avenue, Mosman.*
Water taxi: *to Mosman Rowers Club or Old Cremorne Wharf.*
Amenities: *bar, bike access, carpark, park, phone, picnic tables, playground, sailboard access, seating, shade, toilets, views, walking, wheelchair access.*

Shell Cove Park, Cremorne Point

Top Spot

This **park**, stretching in a narrow strip along the western side of Cremorne Point, is typical of North Shore harbour parks—rock-fringed water on one side, houses on the other and plenty of grass and native vegetation in between. And, of course, excellent **views** of the Sydney skyline.

At the northern end of the park a poor excuse for a beach has dirty water and patchy sand, but **sailboards** can be launched from there. If you enjoy a walk that is neither too strenuous nor too hilly and has plenty of fine views and **picnic** spots, then this could be the place for you. It is possible to **walk** right around Cremorne Point, past the ferry wharf to link up with Harnett Park.

About halfway to the wharf, the MacCallum Pool—a small, fully enclosed harbour **pool**—is open to the public but has neither change sheds nor toilets. If you feel more like sitting than walking, **fishing** is popular from the jetty and along the rocks beside the park as well. The area also offers **seats** and **shade**, and a **phone** at the ferry wharf.

There is adequate parking, however this spot can be reached by bus, ferry and **bike** (although bikes are not allowed on the path). There is also **wheelchair access**.

Ferry: *to Cremorne Wharf.*
Bus: *to Milson Road, Cremorne Point, nos 225 & 226.*
Train: *none.*
Car: *access from Milson Road, Cremorne Point.*
Water taxi: *to Cremorne Wharf.*
Amenities: *bike access, fishing, jetty, park, parking, phone, picnicking, pool, sailboard access, seating, shade, views, walking, wheelchair access.*

Kurraba Point Reserve, Neutral Bay

This flat open **park** is well-grassed and has excellent **views** across the harbour to the city from the two lookouts. However, it has few amenities, no direct access to the water and no shade.

Farthest from the point at the northern end of the reserve, there is a quiet, semi-private area where people sometimes sunbake nude in summer, or enjoy private **picnics** all through the year. People also **fish** over the railing at the edge of the water and from the nearby Kurraba ferry wharf. There is a shop nearby, some **seating** and a modest area for walking.

Parking is available in nearby streets but the area can also be reached by bus and ferry. There is **bike** and **wheelchair access** as well.

Ferry: *to Kurraba Wharf, nearby.*
Bus: *to Hayes Street, nos 225 & 226.*
Train: *none.*
Car: *access from Kurraba Road.*
Water taxi: *to Kurraba Point Wharf, about 200 metres walk.*
Amenities: *bike access, fishing, park, parking, picnicking, seating, views, walking, wheelchair access.*

Death of Joe Lynch

Joe Lynch, a leading figure in the bohemian subculture of Sydney during the 1920s, left Circular Quay on the Mosman ferry Kiandra at 7.45 pm on Saturday, 14 May 1927. Bound for a party at Mosman, his pockets, according to legend, were loaded with beer bottles. As the ferry passed Fort Denison a man saw Joe in the water and jumped in to save him. Lynch resisted his efforts and sank, never to be seen again.

Neutral Bay Wharf, Neutral Bay

Although it is tiny, the **park** just next to this wharf is pretty and has **views** across the busiest part of the harbour toward Garden Island and Elizabeth Bay. A short distance to the west, along a boardwalk past the Australian Customs buildings, lies a bonus smidgin of green.

The wharf park offers **seating** and **shade**, a **phone** and **picnic tables**. The minuscule **beach** is difficult to find, although it can be seen from High Street, North Sydney. **Sailboards** could be launched from here. **Fishing** is a popular pastime from the park itself.

A tiny **parking** area is available but the spot can be reached by bus and, of course, by ferry. There is **bike** and **wheelchair access**.

Ferry: *to Neutral Bay Wharf.*
Bus: *to Hayes Street Wharf, nos 225 & 226.*
Train: *none.*
Car: *access from Hayes Street, Neutral Bay.*
Water taxi: *to Neutral Bay Wharf.*
Amenities: *beach, bike access, carpark (tiny), fishing, jetty, park, phone, picnic tables, sailboard access, seating, shade, views, wheelchair access.*

Anderson Park, Neutral Bay

Flat, grassy and open, this largish **park** is much used by local people. One of its finest features is the huge old Moreton Bay figs that line both sides of the park, blocking out the high-rise buildings and providing a feeding ground at night for flying foxes.

Neutral Bay can also claim a spot in Australia's early colonial history. This was the bay where ships from nations neutral in the Napoleonic Wars—waged between 1805 and 1815 by France against England, Prussia, Austria and Russia—were allowed to berth. It is also the bay from which Charles Kingsford Smith flew out on his historic first crossing of the Pacific Ocean.

Today, the feeling of open space is refreshing in such a heavily built-up area—this is a place for running about with frisbees or playing ball games. For the truly **sport**-minded there are even cricket nets, and **fishing** is popular over the harbour wall. The park also offers plenty of room for **walking** and lots of **shade** as well as **seating** and a **playground** for children.

Very little **parking** is available, but the area can be reached by bus and as it is so flat it has good **bike** and **wheelchair access**.

Ferry: *to Neutral Bay Wharf, not far away.*
Bus: *to Kurraba Road, nos 225 & 226.*
Train: *none.*
Car: *access from Kurraba Road or Clark Road.*
Water taxi: *to Neutral Bay wharf, about half a kilometre away.*
Amenities: *bike access, fishing, parking, park, phone, playground, seating, shade, sport, toilets, views, walking, wheelchair access.*

Kesterton Park, North Sydney

This modest **park**, built around the High Street ferry wharf, serves the surrounding residential area. It is a lovely place to stroll in the sun, taking in the **views** of the submarine base and the high-rise towers around Neutral Bay

A childrens' **playground**, **picnic tables** and **toilets** combine with enough **seating** and **shade** to make this a good spot for a comfortable picnic, but there are also some private places in which to think or read. The park is blessed: the picnic tables are sheltered and the area is also large enough and flat enough for ball games. Sailboarding is illegal in this part of the harbour from North Sydney Wharf south to Elizabeth Bay.

There is no carpark and street **parking** spaces are almost impossible to find, so it is best to approach this park on foot or by bus or ferry. The park is both **bike** and **wheelchair accessible**.

Ferry: *to Neutral Bay wharf.*
Bus: *to Kurraba Road, nos 225 & 226.*
Train: *none.*
Car: *access from High Street, North Sydney.*
Water taxi: *to Neutral Bay wharf.*
Amenities: *bike access, jetty, park, parking (limited), picnic tables, playground, seating, shade, toilets, views, walking, wheelchair access.*

Milson Park, North Sydney

Milson Park at the head of Careening Cove is large and flat with grassy, open spaces. Beautiful old Moreton Bay figs are a special feature of the area, providing plenty of **shade** and attracting mobs of flying foxes at night. The cove itself was named for the use to which it was put in early colonial times when Captain Arthur Phillip careened, or cleaned, his ship in the shallow waters of the bay.

The **park** has plenty of room for a pleasant stroll and the densely packed spreading trees mean it is cool even on a very warm day. A popular spot for families, lovers or elderly people taking the air, there are **picnic tables** and **toilets** as well as a childrens' **playground**, **seating** and a **phone**. People **fish** from the harbour wall and **sailboards** can be launched from the **boat ramp**, but can be used only close to shore.

Fine restaurants with water views can be found at the nearby Ensemble Theatre and the Sydney Flying Squadron yacht club. The Ensemble Theatre, one of Sydney's oldest subscription theatres, produces plays throughout the year and is well worth a visit.

While there is street **parking**, the area is well served by public transport. The park is **bike** and **wheelchair accessible**.

Ferry: *to High Street Wharf, a 10-minute walk away at Kesterton Park, North Sydney.*
Bus: *to nearby Clark Road, Milsons Point, no. 263.*
Train: *North Shore line to Milsons Point, and a 10-minute walk.*
Car: *access from McDougall Street.*
Water taxi: *to the Ensemble Theatre or the Sydney Flying Squadron.*
Amenities: *bike access, boat ramp, fishing, park, parking phone, picnic tables, playground, sailboard access, seating, shade, toilets, walking, wheelchair access.*

Beulah Street Wharf and Park, Kirribilli

This small but attractive **park** around Beulah Street **ferry** wharf is no more than a strip of grass between two blocks of flats, but it has some rather nice **views** of the Sydney skyline and a seat from which to enjoy them. It is well **shaded** by the buildings and slopes fairly steeply, with steps to the water. The other chief attraction is **fishing**, which is carried on despite the signs declaring it illegal.

This tiny park can be reached by all forms of public transport, but many steps make it inaccessible by wheelchair.

Ferry: *to Beulah Street Wharf.*
Bus: *to North Sydney, a 15-minute walk.*
Train: *North Shore Line to Milsons Point, and a 10-minute walk.*
Car: *access from Beulah Street, Kirribilli.*
Water taxi: *to Beulah Street Wharf.*
Amenities: *fishing, park, seating, shade, views.*

The George Dean (or Lemon Syrup) Case

In 1895 George Dean, a ferry captain on the Mosman route, was accused of attempting to poison his wife with arsenic and strychnine, commonly available at the time. They both loved lemon syrup and he was supposed to have added these poisons to their syrup. The case aroused much public hysteria, with most people—fuelled by John Norton's ***Truth*** *newspaper—originally on the side of Dean. He was found guilty but public concern led to a Commission of Enquiry, which eventually released Dean from prison, whereupon he became a tourist attraction on his ferry.*

His lawyer, Richard Meagher, later stated that Dean had confessed to him, following which a chemist said that he had sold poison to Dean, who was re-arrested with public opinion now angrily against him. After many twists and turns, his conviction was eventually quashed on technical grounds by the Full Court and after his release he was never seen again.

Mary Booth Park, Kirribilli

This elevated **park**, complete with a lookout that commands breathtaking **views** across to the city skyline and the Sydney Harbour Bridge, links up with Bradfield Park to form a solid area of green space all the way to Lavender Bay on the western side of the bridge.

There is a large flat grassed area, suitable for childrens' games or **picnicking**, with well-sheltered **picnic tables** and some steep slopes down to where trees line the path along the water's edge. Some people come here to **fish**. This park has been under development for a while and the construction of a linking **walk** around to Lavender Bay is progressing nicely.

While there is only street parking, this spot is well-served by public transport, including water taxis and ferries from Jeffrey Street Wharf, located on the eastern side of the harbour bridge at Milsons Point. The park can be accessed by **bike** and, at its upper reaches, by **wheelchair**.

Ferry: *to Jeffrey Street Wharf or nearby Beulah Street Wharf.*
Bus: *to North Sydney or Milsons Point, nos 228, 229, 230.*
Train: *North Shore Line to Milsons Point.*
Car: *access from Waruda Street, Kirribilli.*
Water taxi: *to Jeffrey Street Wharf.*
Amenities: *bike access, fishing, park, picnic tables, seating, shade, views, walking, wheelchair access.*

Bradfield Park, Milsons Point

A large sloping grassy **park** under the Sydney Harbour Bridge, this is a popular area for lunchtime ball games, strolling or just taking in the **view** of the city. Most spectacular, perhaps, is the perspective you get of the bridge itself—the sight of the surprisingly vast underbelly makes you appreciate this incredible feat of engineering.

At lunchtime, office workers play touch football and joggers circle the park or run through it on their way from Lavender Bay or Mary Booth Park. A tree-planting program is in place to reduce the bareness of the park; meanwhile **picnic tables**, a childrens' **playground** and a **rotunda** make this a comfortable spot for a quick escape from the city. Of course, cars on the Bridge and the Harbour Tunnel ventilation shafts mean this is not the quietest of places, and the air can be less than fresh. There is plenty of **seating**, including a couple of sandstone buildings with seats and some shaded concrete tables. There's room for **walking**, a **phone** and **shade** from the bridge itself. This is also a popular **fishing** spot.

The area has street **parking** (metered) though most of the time spaces are hard to find, but plenty of public transport nearby means access is not a problem. The park is also **bike** and **wheelchair accessible**.

Ferry: *to Jeffrey Street Wharf.*
Bus: *to Milsons Point, nos 228, 229, 230.*
Train: *North Shore Line to Milsons Point Station.*
Car: *access via Jeffrey Street.*
Water taxi: *to Jeffrey Street Wharf.*
Amenities: *bike access, fishing, park, parking, phone, picnic tables, playground, rotunda, seating, shade, views, walking, wheelchair access.*

Sydney Harbour Bridge to Iron Cove Bridge, North Side

West of the Sydney Harbour Bridge the harbour foreshores take on a more intimate quality as the northern and southern shores draw together around the Lane Cove and Parramatta rivers. The suburbs here in this 'working end' of the harbour are among the oldest in Sydney and are fairly high density, which makes some of the rugged bushland parks a pleasant surprise.

This section stretches from the bridge to Greenwich Point then skips over the Lane Cove River to Woolwich before exploring the lower reaches of the Parramatta River to the Iron Cove Bridge. Located as they often are down narrow winding roads heading for the water's edge, some of the parks in this section are not always easy to find. The effort, however, is usually worthwhile because many of them are near empty much of the time. Some of the better parks in the area, such as Balls Head Reserve, Waverton, or Kellys Bush Reserve, Woolwich, have superb harbour views.

The North Sydney Olympic Pool is a superb facility where swimming affords a spectacular view of the CBD and it is worth a visit.

SYDNEY HARBOUR BRIDGE TO IRON COVE BRIDGE, NORTH SIDE.

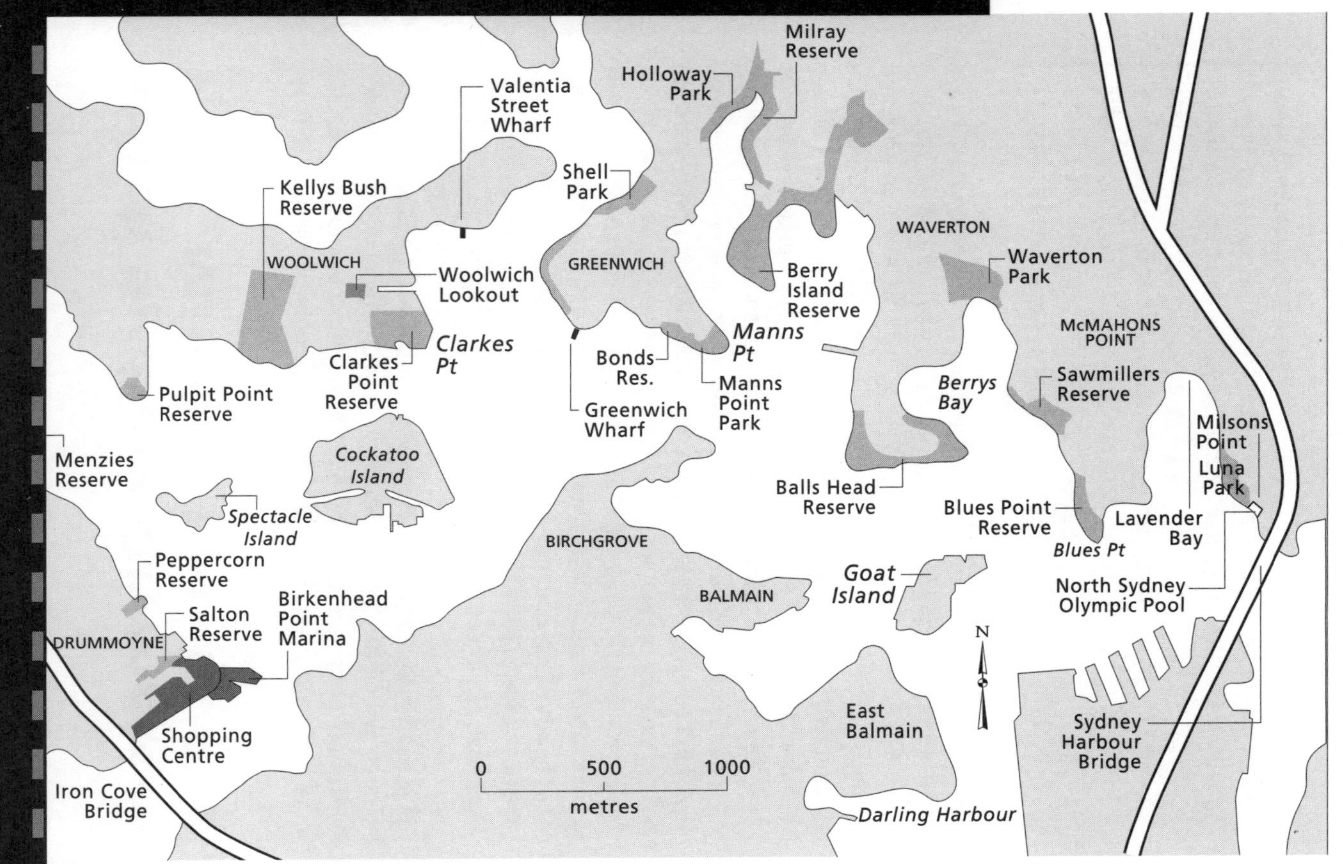

North Sydney Olympic Pool, Milsons Point

Many of Australia's champion swimmers, including Dawn Fraser, have trained and competed in this fabulous outdoor Olympic-sized saltwater pool. Nestling under the Harbour Bridge on the eastern shore of Lavender Bay, the pool offers spectacular **views** across the water toward the city and Darling Harbour.

This fine old 1950s Sydney institution has been beautifully maintained. Some of the nicer features of the pool are the sheltered alcoves on the harbour side, with glass walls facing the water, where couples or family groups congregate. Although some of the lanes will often be occupied by serious lap swimmers, you can usually find space in the water for a frolic.

Heated in winter and with a giant plastic 'bubble' to fend off the chill, the pool is also equipped with spas, **toilets**, a kiosk—opening out to the general public as well as to those in the pool—and sunbathing areas. Within the pool grounds there is a **phone** as well as **picnic tables**, **seating** and **shade**. Just outside the pool grounds a boardwalk runs around the pool, past the old Luna Park toward the head of Lavender Bay and **fishing** is very popular from the **jetty** here. There is also a childrens' **playground** in nearby Bradfield Park.

Street parking is modest but there is plenty of public transport. The pool also has **bike** and **wheelchair access**.

Ferry: *to Milsons Point Wharf.*
Bus: *to Milsons Point, nos 228, 229 & 230.*
Train: *North Shore Line to Milsons Point.*
Car: *access from Broughton Street, Milsons Point.*
Water taxi: *to Milsons Point Wharf.*
Amenities: *bike access, fishing, history, jetty, park, parking (metered), phone, picnic tables, playground, pool, seating, shade, toilets, views, walking, wheelchair access.*

Lavender Bay, McMahons Point

Surprisingly quiet for a location so close to bustling North Sydney, the **park** at the head of this peaceful bay is flat, open and grassy beside the water but steeply sloping behind. The **beach** is very small but pleasant and swimmable, and there is plenty of **seating** and **shade** just back from the water.

Views across the harbour toward the city, Darling Harbour, Pyrmont and Balmain are excellent and there is plenty of **walking** to be had on a boardwalk past the old Luna Park. The boardwalk eventually joins a footpath that curves around the bay to Lavender Bay Park and the street where painter Brett Whiteley once lived. The bay also offers fine dining at Sails Restaurant, near McMahons Point. **Fishing** is very popular along the boardwalk and on the three **jetties**, despite the signs. There is also a **boat ramp** near the wharf.

Parking is hard to find, but there is a free (1 hour) carpark and street parking at Lavender Crescent. Public transport is plentiful and not too far away. There is **bike** and **wheelchair access** to the park and along the boardwalk.

Ferry: *to Milsons Point Wharf.*
Bus: *nos 228, 229 & 230 around the corner at the North Sydney Olympic Pool.*
Train: *North Shore Line to Milsons Point.*
Car: *access from Glen Street, North Sydney.*
Water taxi: *to Sails Restaurant, McMahons Point.*
Amenities: *beach, bike access, boat ramp, fishing, history, jetty, park, parking (limited) seating, shade, toilets, views, walking, wheelchair access.*

Blues Point Reserve, McMahons Point

It is the magnificent views of the Harbour Bridge and the Sydney skyline that give this popular park its charm. Extended families often gather here for large **picnics** and ball games and the grass is frequently covered with children scampering around.

The beach is tiny, but the childrens **playground** is much used, and there is enough space to take a gentle stroll. The 1928 ferry depot, just beside the park at the end of Blues Point Road, is now a museum devoted to the history of the area. There are **toilets**, **seating** and plenty of **shade** from the trees scattered through the **park**. People often enjoy **fishing** from the **jetty** and point.

Parking is a bit tight, but this spot can also be reached by ferry, bus and water taxi. It is a pleasant downhill walk along Blues Point Road from North Sydney Station, and the return climb can be eased by stopping at one of the numerous charming outdoor cafes along this road. There is also **bike** and **wheelchair access** to the park.

Ferry: *to McMahons Point Wharf, beside the park.*
Bus: *to Blues Point, no. 267.*
Train: *to North Sydney Station, then a downhill walk of about one and a half kilometres.*
Car: *access from Blues Point Road, McMahons Point.*
Water taxi: *to McMahons Point Wharf.*
Amenities: *bike access, fishing, history, jetty, park, parking, picnicking, playground, toilets, seating, shade, views, walking, wharf, wheelchair access.*

Sawmiller Reserve, McMahons Point

Despite the comparative lack of amenities, Sawmiller Reserve has a wonderful atmosphere and is a very relaxing place to visit. Well-treed, grassy and open, this **park** is very large indeed—the more you **walk**, the more new sections open up before you.

Once the site of a large timber export depot with wooden buildings on poles stretching out over the water, the area became a park when the depot moved elsewhere. The reserve has designated **picnic** areas and rewarding **views** across Berrys Bay. The locals might like to keep it all to themselves but it is a marvellous spot for a quiet event—a Sunday picnic, perhaps—or even the office Christmas party. Joggers run through the park regularly, mostly in the early mornings or evenings and, although the access is steepish, it is flat enough to be enjoyed by **bicycle**, and is also suitable for **wheelchairs**.

Public transport and parking are both extremely limited.

Ferry: *none.*
Bus: *along Woolcott Street, no. 267.*
Train: *none.*
Car: *access from West Crescent, McMahons Point.*
Water taxi: *none.*
Amenities: *bike access, fishing, history, jetty, park, picnic tables, shade, views, walking, wheelchair access.*

Sydney Harbour Bridge

The 'Coathanger' was under construction for eight years before opening in 1932. During this time it was called the 'Iron Lung' because of the number of men it kept in work during the Great Depression period. Just as the bridge was to be officially opened by Jack Lang, then premier of NSW, Captain de Groot, leader of a right wing movement called the New Guard, rode up and cut the ribbon early as a protest against Lang.

Waverton Park, Waverton

This grassy **park** on Berrys Bay is quite pleasant and spacious. Steeply sloping in places, open in others, the **views** across the water toward Goat Island and Balmain are respectable.

The small **beach** is reasonable but not a great deal used. People seem to prefer **fishing** to swimming at this park. There is also a childrens' **playground** and a **phone** at the adjacent bowling club. With ample **seating** and **shade**, the park is also large enough for a decent stroll.

For all that, this place lacks atmosphere. Visitors who are looking for somewhere off the beaten track might find it attractive for a private open-air function or quiet **picnic** with friends or family. And there is plenty of space for ball games. This is probably more a spot for the locals to catch a quiet breath of fresh air after a hard days' work.

Waverton Park does offer a sizeable **carpark** although public transport is reasonable. There is limited **bike** and **wheelchair access**.

Ferry: *none.*
Bus: *to Woolcott Street, Waverton, no. 267.*
Train: *to Waverton.*
Car: *access from Woolcott Street, Waverton.*
Water taxi: *none.*
Amenities: *beach, bike access (limited), carpark, fishing, park, phone, picnic tables, playground, seating, shade, toilets, views, walking, wheelchair access (limited).*

Balls Head Reserve

Top Spot

Balls Head Reserve is a breath of fresh air in the crowded, high-density Lower North Shore. The elevated peninsula is covered with bushland and has excellent **walking** tracks right around the perimeter. There are superb **views** from many vantage points, and Aboriginal rock carvings can be found on some of the rocks.

This is the perfect park for a family **picnic**, an outdoor wedding or an hour's relaxed bushwalking (see the Walks section, page 175). **Seating** and **shade** abound and, while there is not a great deal of open lawn, there are some lovely **picnic** spots atop rocks, most offering harbour views. There are also plenty of **picnic tables** and **barbecues**, a well-equipped childrens' **playground** and a **toilet block**. Below the bush on the western side of the peninsula is a small **beach**, a little polluted from nearby industrial facilities, and **fishing** is popular from some parts of the foreshore. For a taste of **history**, the old Quarantine Station on the eastern side of the park is now a museum.

The **carpark** is free and huge and this is just as well since transport is limited. You can also access the area by **bike**, and the picnic area is **wheelchair accessible**.

Ferry: *none.*
Bus: *267 along Woolcott Street but it is a fair walk.*
Train: *Waverton Station and a walk of about one kilometre.*
Car: *access from Balls Head Road, Waverton.*
Water taxi: *none.*
Amenities: *barbecues, beach, bike access, carpark, fishing, history, park, picnic tables, playground, seating, shade, toilets, views, walking, wheelchair access (limited).*

Berry Island Reserve, Wollstonecraft

Top Spot

Very similar to nearby Balls Head, this peninsular **park** is a restful bush haven from the stresses of urban life. Here you can enjoy a large flat open grassy area or stroll through elevated natural bushland, enjoying harbour **views** across the water to Birchgrove—a walker's paradise but also a paradise for bush poets, thinkers...or lovers.

Surprisingly wild in an otherwise built-up area, possums and owls are plentiful here and can often be spotted at night. The beach is small and disappears at high tide, but there are quite a few lovely **picnic** areas. A **playground** for children, lots of **shade** and some **seating**—though no picnic tables—fills out the picture of a mainly bush park left pretty much to nature, although there is a **toilet** block. People enjoy **fishing** from the rocks around the peninsula.

There is **bike access** and limited **wheelchair access** (to the grassy roadside area only). While Berry Island is a significant walk from Wollstonecraft station on the North Shore Line, there is some **parking** on Shirley Road.

Ferry: *none.*
Bus: *to Wollstonecraft Station, no. 265.*
Train: *to Wollstonecraft Station.*
Car: *access from Shirley Road.*
Water taxi: *none.*
Amenities: *bike access, fishing, park, parking, picnicking, playground, seating, shade, toilets, views, walking, wheelchair access (limited).*

Holloway Park, Greenwich

On the eastern side of Berry Island, Holloway **Park** with its natural **bush** areas and grassy spots is a good park for walking or for finding quiet spots to meditate, but there are no amenities.

Entrance to the park is via Vista Street, and it gives good **views** across to Berry Island Reserve.

There is a lovely walking **track** from Vista Street to Berry **Creek**, from which you can walk up the valley to Wollstonecraft Station or around the bay to the south through Milray **Reserve** and to Berry Island, where you will find toilets and a playground. At the opposite end of the park is the Shell Gore Bay Terminal.

Holloway Park and Milray Reserve are fairly quiet areas, and parking can usually be found in surrounding streets.

Ferry: *none.*
Bus: *to Wollstonecraft Station, no. 265.*
Train: *to Wollstonecraft Station.*
Car: *access from Vista Street.*
Water taxi: *none.*
Amenities: park, shade, views, walking.

Manns Point Park, Greenwich

This elevated **park** may be **small** but it has a lovely feel about it. Lots of open grassy space, small areas of natural bushland and great **views** almost overcome the fact that it is right next to a huge oil storage depot and dock. Manns Point has a little place in **history** too—it was from this spot that the first telephone cable was laid under Sydney Harbour early this century.

Today, the park has **seating** as well as plenty of **shade** under some beautiful old trees, but no toilets. People also enjoy **fishing** from the rocks below. While **wheelchair access** is limited, the sealed paths in the park enable a wheelchair-bound person to take in the full pleasure of the view. There is just enough room for a pleasant **stroll**, which can be extended by following a pleasant unsealed waterside pathway to Bonds Reserve and the Greenwich Sailing Club a short distance to the west.

Though the park is far too small to ride a bike in, it is accessible by bike and while parking is limited, this is one of the few places on Sydney Harbour where you can enjoy views from your car.

Ferry: *to Greenwich Wharf, a few streets away.*
Bus: *to Greenwich Wharf, nos 265 & 266.*
Train: *none.*
Car: *access from Prospect Street, Greenwich.*
Water taxi: *to Greenwich Wharf, a few streets away.*
Amenities: *bike access, fishing, history, park, parking (limited), seating, shade, views, walking, wheelchair access (limited).*

Bonds Reserve, Greenwich

This small, pleasant, flat **park** beside the Greenwich Sailing Club is beloved by anglers who **fish** over the wall. The reserve has a small **beach**, not much used, and modest **views** across this narrowest part of the harbour to Birchgrove.

The reserve was named after the original Bond Store that once stood here, although nothing now remains. Today, the large old trees and rock wall add to the spot's charm and help make it a pleasant place for **picnicking**. At the eastern end, where the **walk** to Manns Point begins, a medium-sized open grassy area spreads out beneath a cliff. The lucky family group that arrives first can picnic here all day in relative privacy, disturbed by only the occasional passing walker or jogger. The park offers some **seating** and **shade**. A **boat ramp** provides easy **sailboard access** (but bear in mind that sailboarding is forbidden east of Manns Point).

Public transport is quite plentiful but there is also a small **carpark**. The reserve also offers **bike** and **wheelchair access**.

Ferry: *to Greenwich Wharf, not far away.*
Bus: *to Greenwich Wharf, nos 265 & 266.*
Train: *none.*
Car: *access from O'Connell Street, Greenwich.*
Water taxi: *to the jetty.*
Amenities: *beach, bike access, boat ramp, carpark, fishing, history, jetty, park, picnicking, sailboard access, seating, shade, views, walking, wheelchair access.*

Greenwich Wharf and Shell Park, Greenwich

Top Spot At first sight this Greenwich park may seem small, but soon you realise that Shell Park's narrow strip of green stretches all the way along the western side of Greenwich Peninsula. **Shade,** provided by some of the loveliest old trees on the harbour, combines with good **views** and a wide range of amenities to create one of the Harbour's truly top spots. A pretty, pocket-handkerchief sized **beach** lies just east of Greenwich Wharf. Nearby, a childrens' **playground** and an enclosed swimming **pool**—the extremely well-maintained Greenwich Baths—help make this an excellent spot for a family day out. **Picnic tables** can be found near the wharf, and along Shell Park there are some delightful **picnic spots**. There are even some tennis courts close by (200 metres up a hill in another park). There is plenty of **seating** close to the wharf and in the park as well as a **phone**. There is a rough-and-ready **boat ramp**—but only for **sailboards** or boats light enough to be carried. **Fishing** is popular around the Sailing Club and at the wharf, as it is at so many ferry wharves around the harbour.

Public transport is plentiful and the wharf area and the harbourside bushwalk through Shell Park is accessible by **bike**. **Wheelchair access** is restricted to the wharf and its immediate environs.

Ferry: *to Greenwich Wharf.*
Bus: *to Greenwich Wharf at Mitchell Street, nos 265 & 266.*
Train: *none.*
Car: *access from Mitchell Street.*
Water taxi: *to Greenwich Wharf.*
Amenities: beach, *bike access, boat ramp, fishing, jetty, park, phone, picnic tables, playground, pool, sailboard access, seating, shade, toilets, views, walking.*

Woolwich Lookout, Woolwich

The Woolwich Lookout area is a pleasant grassy spot on top of the Woolwich peninsula at the eastern end of Woolwich Road. From here you can see a great deal of the harbour including working docks and the Balmain foreshores as well as the tall towers of downtown Sydney. It is not a truly harbourside **park**, since it lies behind old Water Transport Squadron land, but the lookout and nearby Clarkes Point Reserve may soon function as one large, green harbourside area.

The area has **seating** though not much shade, and there is a **phone**. There is a restaurant and bar at the adjacent hotel as well as **toilets**.

A bus to Valentia Street Wharf (which, like many wharves around the harbour, has patches of green on either side of the wharf itself as well as a playground) runs right past the lookout along Woolwich Road. There is a little street **parking** in the area and the park has **wheelchair** and **bike access**.

Ferry: *to Valentia Street Wharf, less than a kilometre away.*
Bus: *to Valentia Street Wharf, no. 538.*
Train: *none.*
Car: *access from Woolwich Road.*
Water taxi: *none.*
Amenities: *bike access, park, parking (limited), phone, seating, toilets, views, wheelchair access.*

Clarkes Point Reserve, Woolwich

Top Spot This splendid rambling **park**, with its rocky **beach** and pleasant **views** across the water towards Balmain and Rozelle, is undulating, well wooded, pretty and full of amenities. It is a very popular spot for couples and families, and the smell of barbecues on weekends is almost irresistible—so don't envy them, join them!

There is plenty of **seating** and **shade** under the many large trees—some of which are spreading Moreton Bay figs.Wood **barbecues**, **picnic tables** and **toilets** also help to make this a perfect family area. The **beach**, quite large by harbour standards, is full of children in summer.

People **fish** from the harbour wall and there is plenty of room for **walking**, not just strolling, among the trees and over the spacious lawns. The Hunters Hill Sailing Club lies in the adjoining Morts Reserve and there is a **boat ramp**. A **sailboard** could be launched from here, too.

The **carpark** is free, large, and right next to the reserve and there is **bike** and **wheelchair access**.

Ferry: *to Valentia Street Wharf, less than a kilometre away.*
Bus: *to Valentia Street Wharf, no. 538, runs along Woolwich Road a few hundred metres away.*
Train: *none.*
Car: *access from Clarke Road.*
Water taxi: *none.*
Amenities: *barbecues, beach, bike access, boat ramp, carpark, fishing, park, picnic tables, sailboard access, seating, shade, toilets, views, walking, wheelchair access.*

The city of Sydney abuts the harbour, yet it offers many delightful waterside havens.

North Sydney, as seen from the D Page reserve, Dover Heights.

Kirribilli in the early morning with a ferry in the foreground.

McMahons Point wharf makes commuting easy for harbourside dwellers.

A new park and marina grace the foreshore at Pulpit Point, Hunters Hill.

Sydney Harbour Bridge—one of the largest steel arches in the world.

Many Sydney homes, such as these at Birchgrove, have prime waterfront locations.

Sydney's fish markets and one of Doyle's famous seafood restaurants.

Anzac Bridge, once known as Glebe Island Bridge, spans Blackwattle Bay.

Sydney Aquarium at Darling Harbour is well worth a visit.

Dining by the water in the city at Pier One, Dawes Point.

The replica sailing ship, the *Bounty*, moored in Campbells Cove at The Rocks.

Kellys Bush Reserve, Woolwich

Top Spot

This well-developed bushland **park**, mostly covered with trees and dense scrub, has lots of **walking** tracks, good **views** and quite a few lovely hideaway spots for private **picnics.** There are some small open areas on the slope down from the top of the peninsula and a large flat grassy area beside the water.

Named after an early industrialist who bequeathed the land to the council, Kellys Bush was the subject of a famous struggle between the developers and local environmentalists during the 1970s.

Today, the area's bushland character, with plenty of **shady** trees, is complemented by many amenities both there and in adjoining Weil Park, including **barbecues**, **toilets**, a **playground**, **seating**, and **picnic tables**. People **fish** from the rocks and there is **access** for **sailboards**.

There is plenty of street **parking** nearby, **bike access**, and **wheelchair access**.

Ferry: *none.*
Bus: *to Valentia Street Wharf, no. 538, runs along Woolwich Road at the top of the reserve.*
Train: *none.*
Car: *access from many streets around the park including Alfred Street, Woolwich.*
Water taxi: *to the marina at the bottom of Margaret Street, Woolwich.*
Amenities: *barbecues, bike access, fishing, history, jetty, park, parking, picnic tables, playground, sailboard access, seating, shade, toilets, views, walking, wheelchair access.*

Pulpit Point Reserve, Woolwich

Small but pleasant, this elevated little park has superb **views** up and down the harbour. It is also popular for **fishing** and **sailboards** can be launched from here. There are **seats** under **shady** trees down by the water where an easy hour or two can drift by as you read a book or enjoy the passing water traffic.

Privacy is not really possible as some of the neighbouring luxury houses overlook the park quite obtrusively, but there are still pleasant spots to have a **picnic.** Too small for anything but a brief stroll, the park does nevertheless link up with a nearby park in Fern Bay, where a marina is under development at the time of writing.

There is very limited street **parking** and public transport, but this spot can be **accessed** by **bike** or **wheelchair**.

Ferry: *none.*
Bus: *to Valentia Street Wharf, no. 538, runs along Woolwich Road, around a kilometre away.*
Train: *none.*
Car: *access from Le Vesinet Drive, Woolwich.*
Water taxi: *none.*
Amenities: *bike access, fishing, park, sailboard access, seating, shade, views, walking, wheelchair access.*

Menzies Reserve, Drummoyne

Tucked away at the end of a quiet cul-de-sac, this is a tiny but pretty **park**, with several large, **shady** trees and a bright square of grass. There may be little in the way of parking and few amenities, but there is a ferry wharf and some pleasant **views** toward Hunters Hill and Cockatoo Island.

There is just enough room to get away from the bustle of people walking to and from the ferry wharf, so it would be possible to have a peaceful **picnic** here. The reserve also boasts some **seating** and a **phone**. **Sailboards** can be launched from this spot off the ferry wharf and people often **fish** from the jetty.

The park is accessible by **bike** or **wheelchair**.

Ferry: *to Wolseley Street Wharf.*
Bus: *along Victoria Road, Drummoyne, nos 500-510, then a walk of around half a kilometre.*
Train: *none.*
Car: *access from Wolseley Street, Drummoyne.*
Water taxi: *to Wolseley Street Wharf.*
Amenities: *bike access, fishing, jetty, park, picnicking, phone, sailboard access, seating, shade, views, wheelchair access.*

Peppercorn Reserve, Drummoyne

The best part of this two-level park (the levels are separated by a stone wall about a metre and a half high) is hidden from the road by trees, so the lovely parkland beyond the steps is a very pleasant surprise. The combination of open flat grassy space and clusters of shady trees makes this a perfect spot for families or couples wanting to enjoy a private harbourside barbecue or picnic. There are also pleasant **views** toward Cockatoo and Spectacle islands,Woolwich and the city towers in the distance.

The park itself is beautiful, with large, **shady** trees, some **picnic tables** and several ample **barbecues**. Unfortunately, the water on the tiny beach can be filthy. **Fishing** is popular from the harbour wall and **sailboards** can be launched here.

The steps mean the reserve cannot be accessed by bike or wheelchair unless there are some strong people on hand.

Ferry: *to Birkenhead Shopping Centre, 500 metres away.*
Bus: *to Birkenhead Shopping Centre, nos 500-510.*
Train: *none.*
Car: *access from St Georges Crescent, Drummoyne.*
Water taxi: *to Birkenhead Point marina.*
Amenities: *barbecues, fishing, park, parking, picnic tables, sailboard access, seating, shade, views.*

Shipbuilding

The first ship built in Australia was a ferry constructed at Sydney Cove a few months after the First Fleet sailed in. It was built to maintain communications between the Sydney colony and the new farming outpost at Rose Hill, near modern-day Parramatta. The ferry was powered by sail and oar.

Salton Reserve, Drummoyne

Despite being right next door to Birkenhead Point Shopping Centre, this modest **park** can be quiet and almost deserted, apart from the few parked cars encroaching on the grass. The old spreading trees, which provide plenty of **shade**, are a particularly attractive feature.

There is **seating** and, while the reserve may not be enormous, it is large enough for a pleasant stroll to take the air and enjoy the modest **views** across to Cockatoo Island, Spectacle Island and Woolwich. There are even a couple of spots where you can get off the beaten track and contemplate the water undisturbed.

Fishing is popular here and a **sailboard** could be launched, although the water is quite dirty because of local industrial waste and prevailing tidal and wind patterns.

The Drummoyne Sailing Club is just next to the reserve on the northern side, but non-members wishing to visit the club should phone first or ask permission from members.

While there are plenty of covered **carparks** at Birkenhead, public transport is plentiful and the park can be **accessed** by **bike** or **wheelchair**.

Ferry: *to Birkenhead Shopping Centre.*
Bus: *to Birkenhead Shopping Centre, nos 500-510.*
Train: *none.*
Car: *access from St Georges Crescent, Drummoyne.*
Water taxi: *to Birkenhead Point marina.*
Amenities: *bike access, carpark, fishing, park, sailboard access, seating, shade, views, walking, wheelchair access.*

Birkenhead Point Shopping Centre, Drummoyne

More welcoming than your average shopping mall, this charming centre was created from the bare bones of an old factory. On the upper 'decks' many smart restaurants, little cafes and a collection of large wholesale retail outlets specialising in furniture, homewares and clothing make the most of the striking **views** toward Cockatoo Island, Balmain and the working end of the harbour. Downstairs the lower 'decks' accommodate a large fresh fruit and vegetable mart, as well as bookshops and other small specialty stores.

The atmosphere is not unlike that of Fishermens Wharf in San Francisco, with lots of open air **seating** on long **shady** verandah-covered decks. A huge marina, including a **boat ramp**, is attached to the complex, which also offers a childrens' **playground**, **toilets**, a **jetty**, boats for **hire**, and **phones**.

There are multistorey covered **carparks** within easy walking of the main building, but public transport is also plentiful. The centre is also accessible by **bike** and **wheelchair**.

Fishing and dogs are prohibited.

Ferry: *to Birkenhead Shopping Centre.*
Bus: *to Birkenhead Shopping Centre, nos 500-510.*
Train: *none.*
Car: *access from Roseby Street, Drummoyne.*
Water taxi: *to Birkenhead Point marina.*
Amenities: *bike access, boat hire, boat ramp, carpark, history, jetty, phones, playground, seating, shade, toilets, views, wheelchair access.*

Iron Cove Bridge to Pyrmont

Until recently this area consisted of low-rise working class residential housing, much of it terraces, interspersed with factories and ferry- or boat-industry sites on the water. Today, suburbs such as Birchgrove and Balmain are among the most sought after in Sydney and many former industrial sites along the water's edge—such as Mort Bay Park, Birchgrove, and Bicentennial Park, Glebe—have been transformed into much-needed inner-city green space.

Most of the parks along this stretch of the harbour are fairly small and, perhaps because Leichhardt Council does not have the funds available to wealthy North Shore councils, some are not very well equipped. They are often pretty, however, and make up for in charm what they lack in size. Many, such as Elkington Park, Balmain, are characterised by beautiful old trees and lots of high ground and slopes, and are surrounded by century-old houses. Yurulbin Park at Yurulbin Point, Birchgrove, is another gem, with its old harbour wall, substantial trees, panoramic views of the entire 'working end' of the harbour, and grassy open areas.

Like those west of the harbour bridge on the north side many of the parks in this section are not easy to find. This means they are often pleasantly private places in which to picnic because of their comparative peace and quiet and are well worth seeking out.

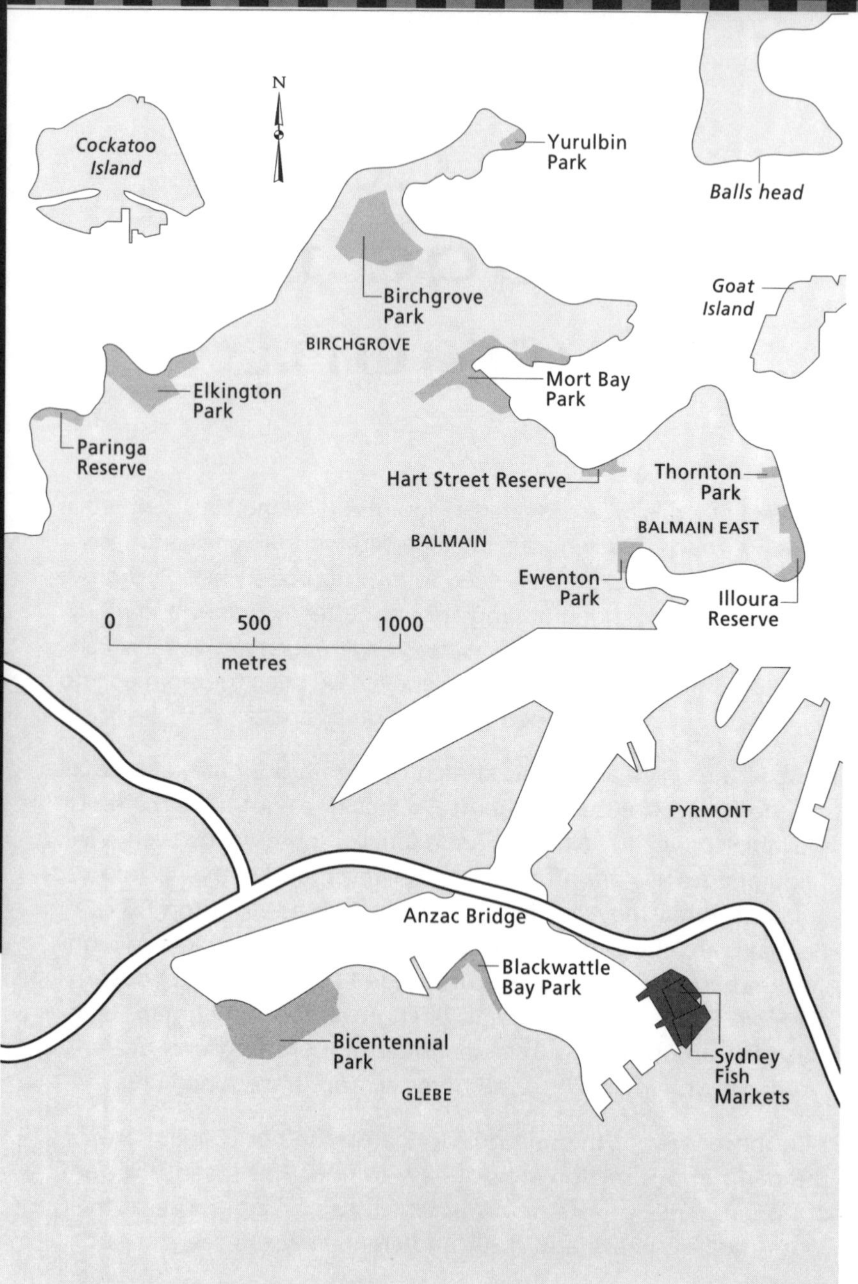

Cockatoo Island
N
Yurulbin Park
Balls head
Birchgrove Park
Goat Island
BIRCHGROVE
Mort Bay Park
Elkington Park
Paringa Reserve
Hart Street Reserve
Thornton Park
BALMAIN EAST
BALMAIN
Ewenton Park
Illoura Reserve
0
500
1000
metres
PYRMONT
Anzac Bridge
Blackwattle Bay Park
Bicentennial Park
Sydney Fish Markets
GLEBE

Paringa Reserve, Balmain

This small **park** is low lying, rectangular and flat—a grassy open area beside the water overshadowed by apartments and with just a few trees. The main attraction here is the charming **cafe** at the ferry wharf. It serves excellent snacks and coffee, and you can enjoy the **view** through its large windows.

People **fish** from the **jetty** and there is some **seating** but only a little **shade**. Only street parking is available and on weekends there's a lot of competition. The area can be accessed by **bike** or **wheelchair**, but there are no paths inside the park.

Ferry: *to Elliott Street Wharf.*
Bus: *along Darling Street, a kilometre away, no. 440.*
Train: *none.*
Car: *access from Elliott Street, Balmain.*
Water taxi: *to Elliott Street Wharf.*
Amenities: *bike access, fishing, jetty, park, seating, some shade, views, wheelchair access.*

Elkington Park, Balmain

Top Spot

Famous as the location of the Dawn Fraser Pool—one of the last of the old-fashioned wooden public pools that once dotted the harbour foreshores—this attractive **park** is ideal for a family **picnic**. The **pool** is named after and was used by the Australian Olympic swimming champion who grew up here in Balmain. The park is elevated and hilly with open grassy areas, plenty of **shade** under the scattered trees and terrific **views** across the harbour to Cockatoo and Spectacle islands.

There is also plenty of **seating** and a **picnic table** as well as a **rotunda** on the elevated part of the park some distance from the water, a kiddies' **playground**, and a pretty formal garden. A **phone** and **kiosk** (at the pool) and a **toilet** block help make this well-appointed park a comfortable place for a day out.

People enjoy **fishing** from the **jetty** and there is space for an extended stroll. The park can be **accessed** by **bicycle**, and there is some street **parking**. The park's hilly nature makes it not ideal for wheelchairs but it is **wheelchair accessible** and there are sealed paths.

Ferry: *to Elliott Street Wharf.*
Bus: *along Darling Street, a kilometre away, no. 440.*
Train: *none.*
Car: *access from White Street, Balmain.*
Water taxi: *to the jetty area at the pool.*
Amenities: *bike access, fishing, jetty, kiosk, park, parking, phone, picnic table, playground, pool, rotunda, seating, shade, toilets, views, walking, wheelchair access.*

Yurulbin Park, Balmain

Pleasant and relaxing, this well-kept two-level **park** on the very end of Yurulbin Point features marvellous **views** across to the North Shore and east to the Harbour Bridge and the city skyline.

Yurulbin is quiet and out-of-the-way with many trees providing plenty of **shade**, some pretty picnic spots and **seating**.

Sailboarding is forbidden east of this point, but **fishing** is popular from the ferry wharf and the park is just long enough for a brisk **walk**. There is only limited **parking**, but the area is accessible by **bike** although some of the slopes may be a bit steep for wheelchair access.

Ferry: *to Yurulbin Point–Birchgrove Wharf.*
Bus: *to Yurulbin Point–Birchgrove Wharf, no. 492, operates on weekends only.*
Train: *none.*
Car: *access from Louisa Road, Birchgrove.*
Water taxi: *to Yurulbin Point–Birchgrove Wharf.*
Amenities: *bike access, fishing, jetty, park, parking (limited), seating, shade, views, walking.*

Birchgrove Park, Birchgrove

Birchgrove Park is the largest harbourside **park** in Birchgrove. Extensive enough for a good **walk** and endowed with sporting facilities including an oval and some tennis courts, this sloping, grassy park with lovely old Moreton Bay figs has a few hideaway spots, some pretty **picnic** areas and pleasant **views** across to Balls Head.

An old, well-established park that has served many generations of Balmanians for sport and leisure, this parks seems to us to be closer in spirit to the harbour than many others, perhaps because of the many boats moored close to its **jetty** and harbour wall. A well-made path follows the perimeter of the sloping greens, and there is also a reasonably well equipped children's **playground**, **a phone**, **toilets** and lots of **shade** and **seating** under large old trees.

The oval, surrounded by a picturesque white picket fence, is popular with joggers and the jetty is a magnet for those indulging in a spot of **fishing**. The tiny beach is unswimmable.

The area has a certain amount of street **parking**, and it can be accessed by **bike** or **wheelchair**.

Ferry: *to Mort Bay, half a kilometre away or Yeand Street Wharf.*
Bus: *to Grove Street, nos 432 & 441.*
Train: *none.*
Car: *access from The Terrace, Birchgrove.*
Water taxi: *to the park jetty.*
Amenities: *bike access, fishing, jetty, park, parking, phone, picnicking, playground, seating, shade, toilets, views, walking, wheelchair access.*

Mort Bay Park, Balmain

This relatively new **park** was created on the site of the old Tasmanian ferry terminal (for many years ocean-going car ferries used to ply the route from Sydney to Tasmania), part of which became a new housing estate. The substantial jetty area could be a reference to the area's former glory.

New tree plantings have yet to mature and therefore provide only a little **shade** so far, but the park's open character is refreshing in this built-up area and there is some **seating**. Modest **views** across the water toward Balls Head Reserve.

The park has plenty of room to stretch your legs, and the wonderful wooden **jetty** is a popular **fishing** spot. The area boasts a **parking** area of moderate size, easy **bike access**, and **wheelchair access** on relatively smooth paths.

Ferry: *to Thames Street Wharf, adjacent to the park.*
Bus: *along Darling Street, about a kilometre away, nos 442, 445 & 446; to Birchgrove Park, half a kilometre away, nos 432 & 441.*
Train: *none.*
Car: *access from College Street.*
Water taxi: *to Thames Street Wharf.*
Amenities: *bike access, fishing, jetty, park, parking, seating, shade, views, walking, wheelchair access.*

Hart Street Reserve, East Balmain

Situated beside the old Colgate Palmolive factory, which used to be famous for showering Balmain with soap flakes, this **reserve** is about a hectare in area and mostly flat, but the ground can be rough. It offers some **shade**, **seating** and people **fish** here. It is regularly maintained and a flower garden is located towards the eastern end of the park. It is suitable for a **picnic**—though there are better spots nearby—but there are few amenities.

There is limited street **parking** and **bike access** but no access for wheelchairs.

Ferry: *to Thames Street Wharf at Mort Bay, half a kilometre away.*
Bus: *along Darling Street, half a kilometre up the hill, nos 442, 445 & 446.*
Train: *none.*
Car: *access from Duke Street, Balmain.*
Water taxi: *none.*
Amenities: *bike access, fishing, park, parking (limited), seating, some shade, walking.*

Thornton Park, East Balmain

Situated beside the Darling Street Wharf, this fairly substantial gently sloping **park** is well-managed and grassy with some **shady** trees. Its partly elevated position makes up for any lack of imagination in its square shape, and contributes to the excellence of the harbour **views** across to Goat Island, North Sydney and the city. The comparative lack of trees at the water's edge brings a sense of being closer to the water than in many other harbour parks and the **jetty**, from which people always seem to be **fishing**, is long and well maintained.

There is barely room for a short stroll, but if you really want to step out, the Balmain Historic Trail starts from here (details available from Leichhardt Council, page 158). The park also offers **toilets**, **seating** and a small **playground** with swings. A **picnic table** provides a nice spot to enjoy the views while eating and a **phone** stands right beside the park.There is only two-hour street parking but public transport abounds. There is **wheelchair** and **bike access** to some parts of the park.

Ferry: *to Darling Street Wharf, next to the park.*
Bus: *to Darling Street Wharf, nos 442, 445 & 446.*
Train: *none.*
Car: *access via Darling Street, East Balmain.*
Water taxi: *to Darling Street Wharf, next to the park.*
Amenities: *bike access, fishing, jetty, park, phone, picnic table, playground, seating, shade, toilets, views, wheelchair access.*

Illoura Reserve, East Balmain

Tucked away behind dense colonial housing in the narrow alleyways of East Balmain, this shady, grassy **park** is a delightfully attractive **picnic** area. Numerous trees ensure that there are plenty of private spots to get away from others. Surprisingly quiet and peaceful so close to the bustle of the city, the park offers spectacular sweeping **views** from nearby Goat Island and Blues Point on the North Shore across the whole city skyline to Darling Harbour.

This reserve, created with a bushland character similar to that of Yurulbin Park, Birchgrove, is a breath of fresh air. Yet it is so close to the city you feel you could almost reach across and touch the tall office towers of the Sydney CBD.

There is a small adventure **playground** to use up children's surplus energy, and more than enough space for an extended stroll in this one-hectare-plus area. There is **seating** in the **shade** of the many large, spreading trees, and a wharf that is popular for **fishing**.

You can park your car in a small **carpark** and would have no trouble **accessing** the park by **wheelchair** or **bike**, although there's nowhere to ride inside.

Ferry: *to Darling Street Wharf, 150 metres away.*
Bus: *to Darling Street Wharf, nos 442, 445 & 446.*
Train: *none.*
Car: *access from Weston Street, East Balmain.*
Water taxi: *to Darling Street Wharf, next to the park.*
Amenities: *bike access, carpark, fishing, jetty, park, picnicking, playground, seating, shade, views, walking, wheelchair access.*

Ewenton Park, Balmain

Named after historic Ewenton House, a colonial mansion that still overlooks the **park**, this small but relaxing green space offers modest **views** towards the city.

The reasonably large area of open grass provides somewhere to hit a tennis ball or throw a frisbee and, while there is no real beach to speak of, this is a pleasant out-of-the-way place for a **picnic**.

There are steps down to the water, but some people **fish** here. There may be more attractive or spectacular parks in Balmain but if what you seek is a little quiet and solitude, this could be your best bet in the area.

The area has a very small **parking** area as well as street parking and can also be **accessed** by **bike**. There is a tiny, flat section of the park adjacent to the parking area that could be **accessed** by a person using a **wheelchair**.

Ferry: *none.*
Bus: *along Darling Street, a short walk away, nos 442, 445 & 446.*
Train: *none.*
Car: *access from Jubilee Place, Balmain.*
Water taxi: *none.*
Amenities: *bike access, fishing, park, parking, picnicking, views, wheelchair access (limited).*

Bicentennial Park, Glebe

Top Spot

What a superb example of the park-maker's art! Recently developed, this beautiful grassy green **park**, together with its neighbours Jubilee Park and Federal Park, forms a large open area big enough for a vigorous run or a long walk. Jubilee Park also boasts an oval. The park features rather nice **views** across Rozelle Bay and over towards the new Anzac Bridge (formerly known as Glebe Island Bridge).

With more established spreading trees providing plenty of **shade** in the older sections of the space, new plantings are already showing promise. Plenty of **seating**, **picnic tables** and a **toilet** block make it an ideal family spot in every way. **Fishing** is a popular pastime here.

The jewel of this park, however, is the children's garden—an absolute delight. Its pretty spaces are filled with bushes, trees and flowers and it also incorporates a **playground**.

There is a fair amount of street **parking**, and the park can be **accessed** easily by **wheelchair** or **bike**.

Ferry: *none.*
Bus: *to Glebe Point, nos 431 & 434.*
Train: *none.*
Car: *access from The Crescent, Annandale, or Glebe Point Road, Glebe.*
Water taxi: *to the park jetty.*
Amenities: *bike access, fishing, park, parking, picnic tables, playground, seating, shade, toilets, views, walking, wheelchair access.*

Blackwattle Bay Park, Glebe

Stretching some 300 metres along the shoreline, this green oasis offers a splendid **view** of the new Anzac Bridge and the city skyline across the water, especially in the evening when city lights add their magic. It was opened in 1983, so there are well-grown trees to provide plenty of **shade**. Free electric **barbecues** are provided by the local council as well as some **seating** but, surprisingly, there are no picnic tables. Some people like to **fish** here—sharks have been sighted in the area.

There is a small **playground**, but it's a bit run down. Some street **parking** with no time limits, but the unsealed paths in the park are a bit rough for wheelchairs and not much fun for bikes.

Ferry: *none.*
Bus: *to Glebe Point, nos 431 & 434, 300 metres away.*
Train: *none.*
Car: *access from Leichhardt Street, Glebe Point.*
Water taxi: *none.*
Amenities: *barbecues, fishing, park, parking, playground, seating, shade, views, walking.*

Sydney Fish Markets, Pyrmont

Top Spot This bustling, lively place has more character than most Sydney retail centres. It is at once an old-fashioned market where competing stallholders offer cheap seafood and a modern shopping mart where sophisticated restaurants—including that harbour institution, Doyles—compete for your business.

Apart from places to buy fish there is a deli, a bread shop and a fruit shop, and other food outlets sell drinks or snacks. There is also a pleasant bar. Peters Fish Market offers **boat hire** and another business offers **charter fishing**. There are **phones** and **toilets** as well as **seating** and **umbrella-shaded** outside **tables** and some tiny green spaces behind the wooden promenade where you can sit and eat your takeaway fish and chips. Ironically, perhaps, fishing is not allowed.

A huge **carpark** ensures you will never wait for parking (except at Christmas when the place becomes a war zone) but in any case, public transport is plentiful. This spot is also **wheelchair accessible**.

Ferry: *none.*
Bus: *nos 468, 500 & 501 to Sydney Fish Markets.*
Train: *Sydney Light Rail (tram) to Miller Street or Wattle Street.*
Car: *access from Bank Street, Pyrmont.*
Water taxi: *to Peters Fish Market private jetty.*
Amenities: *boat hire, carpark, charter fishing, phones, picnic tables, seating, shade, toilets, wheelchair access.*

The First Fleet

HMS Sirius and 12 other vessels, under the command of Captain Arthur Phillip, sailed through the heads into Sydney Harbour on 20 January 1788. After investigating the harbour, they settled at what is now Sydney Cove on 26 January, raising the flag to claim the new land for the King.

The City of Sydney

No area of the harbour has seen as much development in recent years as the area from Pyrmont east of the new Anzac Bridge to Sydney Cove, site of the famous Sydney Opera House. This varied stretch of harbour foreshore has become a model for other cities to follow in redeveloping industrial land beside water into intensive-use leisure areas.

First came Darling Harbour—a spectacularly ambitious redevelopment of disused waterside railway yards around Cockle Bay coordinated by the Darling Harbour Development Authority. Then came the City West Project, focussing on the redevelopment of Pyrmont where docks and industrial sites had become derelict as the 'working harbour' continued its inexorable shift to Port Botany. Finally, the redevelopment of Sydney Cove itself, based around the Sydney Opera House and the Overseas Passenger Terminal, crowned the changes in harbourside areas of the city. Parkland, open space, marinas, museums, docks, retail centres and waterside residential complexes now characterise the area.

The Pyrmont precinct, once accommodating wharves, industrial sites and low-cost terrace housing, is emerging as a trendy inner-city district with the Star City Casino at its heart. When the development is finished, in time for the year 2000 Olympic

Games, it will be possible to walk along almost the entire Pyrmont foreshore—mostly through new parklands. Television studios, art galleries, photography studios and film offices occupy former warehouses; many new blocks of apartments are being built and restaurants and cafes are flourishing.

The Darling Harbour area—once a muddy bay of mangroves that evolved into an industrial district of wharves and railway yards after European settlement—today focusses on leisure activities for international tourists and locals alike. Over 200 shops, restaurants and cafes combine with exhibitions and outdoor entertainment to attract more than 13 million people every year. From the Sydney Aquarium and the Australian National Maritime Museum to Tumbalong Park, the newly redeveloped Cockle Bay Wharf and the Chinese Gardens, Darling Harbour has something for everyone.

Past Darling Harbour towards Sydney Cove, the character-filled wharves along Walsh Bay have been home to some of Sydney's major cultural institutions for many years. Sydney's theatre and dance companies as well as temporary festivals and art exhibitions have all been housed in these wonderful old buildings. The recent acceptance of a commercial tender for redevelopment means that Walsh Bay will soon be completely transformed.

East of the Sydney Harbour Bridge, Sydney Cove—with the Circular Quay ferry terminals, railway station and bus terminus—forms the hub of the city. It was here in 1788 that Captain Arthur Phillip first raised the British flag to annex Australia to the Crown. Cadman's Cottage, Australia's oldest building, still stands on the western shore. A pedestrian concourse lined with cafes and restaurants follows the water's edge from the historic Rocks district below the bridge to the Sydney Opera House on Bennelong Point in the east.

Today the whole area from Pyrmont to Sydney Cove is alive and buzzing and undoubtedly one of the most beautiful downtown waterside areas in any city in the world.

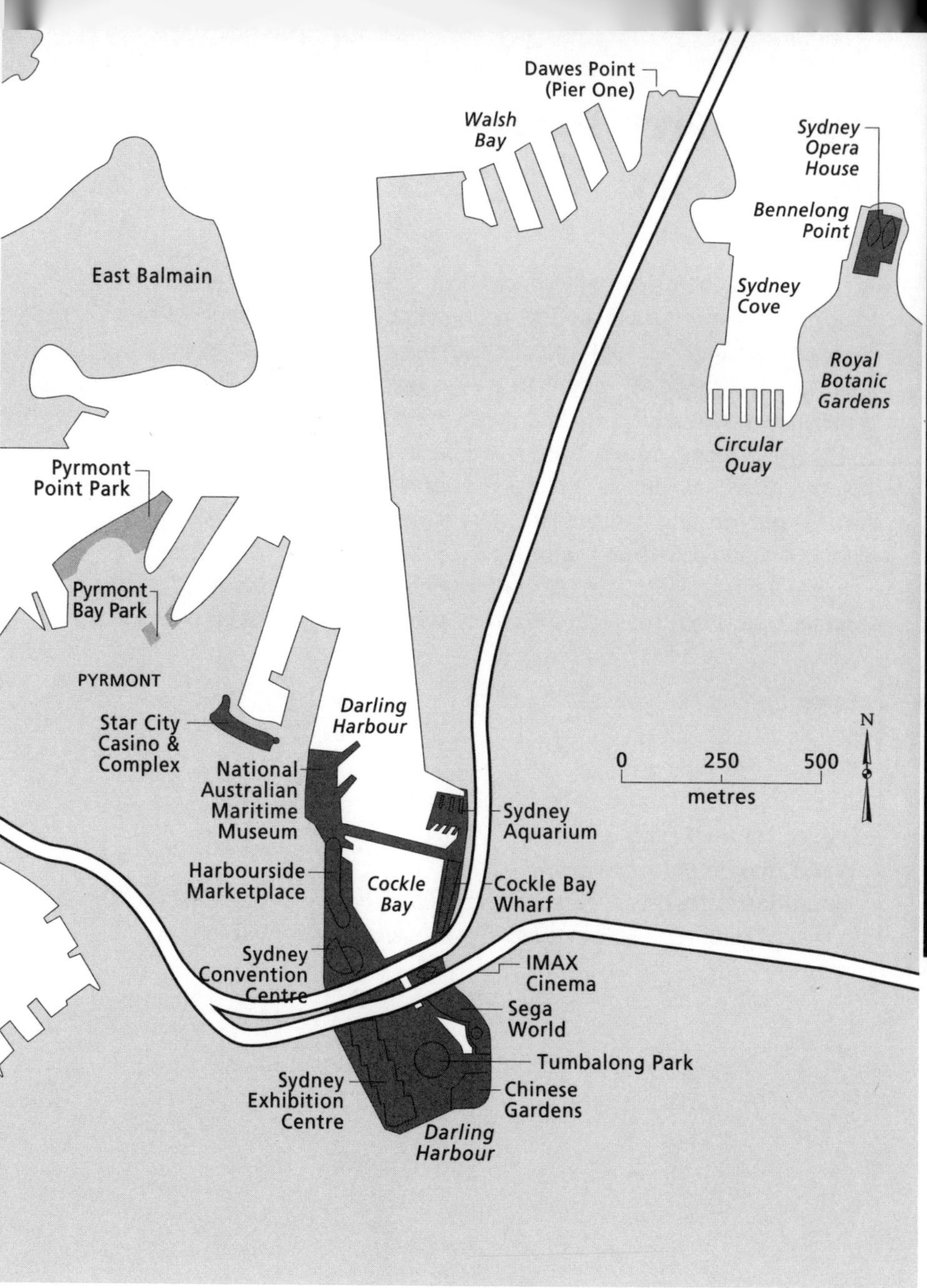

Dawes Point
(Pier One)
Walsh
Bay
Sydney
Opera
House
Bennelong
Point
East Balmain
Sydney
Cove
Royal
Botanic
Gardens
Circular
Quay
Pyrmont
Point Park
Pyrmont
Bay Park
PYRMONT
Darling
Harbour
Star City
Casino &
Complex
National
Australian
Maritime
Museum
0
250
500
metres
N
Sydney
Aquarium
Harbourside
Marketplace
Cockle
Bay
Cockle Bay
Wharf
Sydney
Convention
Centre
IMAX
Cinema
Sega
World
Tumbalong Park
Sydney
Exhibition
Centre
Chinese
Gardens
Darling
Harbour

Pyrmont Point Park, Pyrmont

Jutting out into Johnstons Bay, Pyrmont Point's new one-hectare park occupies a former industrial site and incorporates the area's original wharves. Flat open grassland is dotted with plenty of new, young trees—not yet big enough to provide shade—and there are interesting **views** towards Balmain and across Darling Harbour to the Harbour Bridge and the city.

The park's **picnic tables**, **toilets** and **barbecues** make it a comfortable spot for picnicking. There is also plenty of **seating**, a well-equipped childrens **playground** and **toilets**. There is plenty of room for walking and this is a popular **fishing** spot, too.

While there is plenty of public transport nearby, ample off-street **parking** is provided. The area is **bike** and **wheelchair accessible**.

Ferry: *the Matilda Cruises' 'Rocket' to the Star City Casino, a few hundred metres away.*
Bus: *nos 443, 468 & 888.*
Train: *light rail to Casino, a few hundred metres away.*
Car: *access from Pirrama Road.*
Water taxi: *to the wharves in the park.*
Amenities: *barbecues, bike access, carpark, fishing, jetty, park, picnic tables, playground, seating, toilets, views, walking, wheelchair access.*

Pyrmont Bay Park, Pyrmont

Although not as well positioned as Pyrmont Point Park, this excellent open area allows a bit of breathing space in an otherwise busy precinct. Wedged between the Casino and the Foxtel Studios wharf, the park is grassy, flat and open, with trees not yet fully developed.

While not terribly large, in time this will be a very pretty space and a reasonable **walk** is possible if you don't mind strolling out of the park and along the nearby wharves. There is plenty of **seating** as well as **toilets** although little shade at this stage. People **fish** along the wharves.

Public transport abounds which is just as well as nearby **parking**, while plentiful, is in high demand. There is **bike** and **wheelchair access** to the park.

Ferry: *the Matilda Cruises' 'Rocket' to the Star City Casino, a few hundred metres away.*
Bus: *nos 443 and 468, 888.*
Train: *light rail to Casino, a few hundred metres away.*
Car: *access from Pirrama Road.*
Water taxi: *Water Taxi: to the Foxtel wharf.*
Amenities: *bike access, carpark, fishing, jetty, park, seating, toilets, walking, wheelchair access.*

Cadmans Cottage, West Circular Quay

Dating from 1816, this is one of Sydney's oldest buildings. Originally built for coxswains—masters of the small boats which plied the harbour before good roads were built—it is named after the third coxswain to occupy it, John Cadman. In about 1846 the growing water police made it their headquarters and, when they moved out in 1855, it became a sailors home and later a hostel for visiting merchant ships officers. By the 1960s it had become derelict and in 1972 was declared a Historic Site. Renovation was completed by 1996, and the building is now occupied by the National Parks and Wildlife Service. Originally close to the water's edge, the construction of Circular Quay early this century placed it forty metres from the shoreline.

Darling Harbour

Top Spot

Darling Harbour (Cockle Bay) itself is a modest body of water surrounded on its western, southern and eastern sides by wharves and wide pedestrian concourses, much used for promenading.

The facilities lining the concourse, however, are anything but modest. Ranging from the Australian National Maritime Museum, on the western side of the water, to the Sydney Aquarium on the eastern side—and with many shops, restaurants, cafes and other entertainment facilities in between, including the newly redeveloped Cockle Bay Wharf with its varied restaurants—Darling Harbour offers plenty to see and do. The area also features magnificent **views** of the city skyline.

Street entertainment such as clowns, buskers, jazz bands and jugglers as well as permanent attractions such as the Panasonic IMAX Theatre and Sega World enhance the area's magnetism. Avenues of palms and areas of native plantings create an oasis from the concrete of the nearby city. Two-hectare Tumbalong Park—trees and grass with a children's **playground**—and the Chinese Gardens, opposite the Sydney Exhibition Centre, extend the green space.

There is also plenty of **seating** and **shade**, several large **jetties** and numerous **phones** and **toilets**. **Boats** can be **hired** and many harbour cruises begin here.

While Darling Harbour is linked to the city by pedestrian pathways, there is also a huge **carpark** and it is **bike** and **wheelchair accessible**.

Ferry: *Matilda Cruises run a continuous express ferry, the 'Rocket', to Circular Quay and Pyrmont.*
Bus: *From Circular Quay and Town Hall, no. 443.*
Train: *Sydney Light Rail to any one of four stops—Entertainment Centre, Exhibition Centre, Convention Centre, Australian National Maritime Museum; Sydney Monorail.*
Car: *access to the main carpark from Darling Drive.*
Water taxi: *to any of the jetties or the continuous wharf.*
Amenities: *bike access, boat hire, carpark, cruises, jetty, park, phones, playgrounds, seating, shade, toilets, views, walking, wheelchair access.*

Walsh Bay, Dawes Point

Between Millers Point at the mouth of Darling Harbour and the southern pylon of the Sydney Harbour Bridge, Walsh Bay is home to four wharves and Pier One—all dating back to pre-container shipping days. The **views** from the wharves are superb—of the Harbour Bridge looming to the east and across the harbour to the lower North Shore.

These wharves are currently home to the Sydney Theatre Company and the Sydney Dance Company as well as the Sydney Philharmonia Choir. The Sydney Theatre Company presents plays at two theatres on Pier 3/4 as well as at the Sydney Opera House, while the Sydney Dance Company uses the wharf for rehearsals. At the end of the wharf, the Sydney Theatre Company has a fine restaurant with more marvellous harbour **views**.

Pier One—a commercial enterprise comprising restaurants, bars, cafes and many shops and stalls selling mostly gifts and clothing—is undergoing renovations at the time of writing. The **jetty** is used as a base by a private cruise company.

Just beside Pier One and under the Sydney Harbour Bridge around the base of the southern pylon—Ives Steps Wharf is a popular **fishing** spot, although people also fish from all the wharves in Walsh Bay.

There is plenty of street **parking** behind the wharves, but this spot is also less than a kilometre from Circular Quay in Sydney Cove—the public transport hub of the city.

Ferry: *Matilda Ferries links Millers Point near Pier One with Sydney Cove, Darling Harbour and Pyrmont.*
Bus: *to Millers Point, no. 433; any of the many buses to Circular Quay, less than a kilometre away.*
Train: *to Circular Quay. Car: access from Hickson Road.*
Car: *to Walsh Bay, via Cowper Wharf Roadway; street parking.*
Water taxi: *to Pier One; to the Sydney Theatre Company wharf, Pier 3/4.*
Amenities: *bike access, cruises, fishing, jetty, park, parking, seating, shade, toilets, views, wheelchair access.*

The Western Shore, Sydney Cove

The western shore of Sydney Cove skirts Sydney's historic Rocks district from the Sydney Harbour Bridge to the ferry terminals at Circular Quay.

Under the bridge, a walkway follows the water around to Dawes Point Reserve—a small elevated **park** with lovely old palm trees and fine views across to the Sydney Opera House.

Next to the reserve the Park Hyatt Hotel overlooks a pleasant paved area around Campbells Cove known as Customs Officers Steps—a link to this spot's past service as the new colony's first port. Restaurants with outdoor eating areas line the cove, which is also home to a couple of unusual cruise boats—the replica of Captain Bligh's Bounty and the Sydney Showboat, a glitzy replica of a Mississippi riverboat. The nearby Sydney Cove Terminal is a dock for cruise liners but also contains two fine restaurants with excellent harbour views.

Beyond the terminal lies Cadman's Cottage and the beginning of the wide pedestrian concourse lining Sydney Cove. A two-hectare **park** spreads around the Museum of Contemporary Art. Water taxis and cruise companies use the **jetty** here and the area is a popular **fishing** spot.

There is plenty of **seating** and **shade** on the western shore, although the jacarandas along the concourse have yet to reach their full potential. There are also **toilets** and **phones**.

This area can be fairly congested and **parking** is limited so it is fortunate that Circular Quay is the public transport hub of the city. There is **bike** and **wheelchair access** to most areas.

Ferry: *to Circular Quay.*
Bus: *any of the many buses to Circular Quay.*
Train: *to Circular Quay.*
Car: *access from George Street, Sydney.*
Water taxi: *to various wharves or jetties.*
Amenities: *bike access, boat hire, cruises, fishing, jetty, park, parking, phone, seating, shade, toilets, views, walking, wheelchair access.*

Southern and Eastern Shores, Sydney Cove

Sydney Cove's pedestrian concourse continues from the western shore right past the ferry terminals and elevated railway station of the southern shore to the famous Sydney Opera House on Bennelong Point in the east.

This busy pedestrian walkway is sprinkled with numerous kiosks, sidewalk cafes and a few restaurants. Trees dot the pavement of the eastern promenade, which leads to the Sydney Opera House and ultimately joins the pathway through the Royal Botanic Gardens around Farm Cove to Mrs Macquaries Point. The Sydney Opera House, a symbol of the city to rival the bridge, dominates this quintessentially Sydney spot.

By contrast, the southern shore is filled with working wharves. Here there is plenty of **seating** and **shade**, as well as **phones** and **toilets**. People **fish** from the promenade and stroll past the buskers.

The concourse by the Opera House offers excellent **views** of the bridge and the city skyline and plenty of room to stroll. On weekends there are markets here as well as music on the forecourt.

The Sydney Opera House is by far Australia's best-known performing arts building—host to plays, operas, concerts and festivals. Within and around the building there are magnificent **views** of the harbour, a number of cafes and restaurants, plenty of **seating** and some **shade** under cafe umbrellas. There are also **toilets** and **phones**.

An underground **carpark**, though not cheap, is large and feeds directly into the Opera House. The Opera House is largely **wheelchair accessible**.

Ferry: *to Circular Quay (the ferry terminus), a few hundred metres from the Opera House.*
Bus: *any to Circular Quay; to the Opera House, nos 438, 324, 325.*
Train: *to Circular Quay, a few hundred metres from the Opera House.*
Car: *Opera House underground carpark from Macquarie Street.*
Water taxi: *to Man O' War jetty.*
Amenities: *bike access carpark, fishing, jetty, phone, seating, shade, toilets, views, walking, wheelchair access.*

Sydney Opera House to South Head

This extremely varied and beautiful stretch of the harbour runs from the heart of the city to the rocky escarpments of South Head and includes the entire harbourside foreshore of the exclusive Eastern Suburbs.

Compared to the North Shore, the Eastern Suburbs has fewer parkland areas beside the water and very little native bushland. By way of compensation fine restaurants, antique shops, cafes, bookshops and boutiques lie within a stone's throw of the many delightful coves and beaches.

Some of the best parks and beaches may not be the biggest—McKell Park, out on the end of high-density Darling Point, might be tiny but it is a top spot with spectacular views up and down the harbour. Way out on South Head, part of the Sydney Harbour National Park, the wind will whip the cobwebs away as you feast your eyes on exhilarating views up and down the harbour and out to sea.

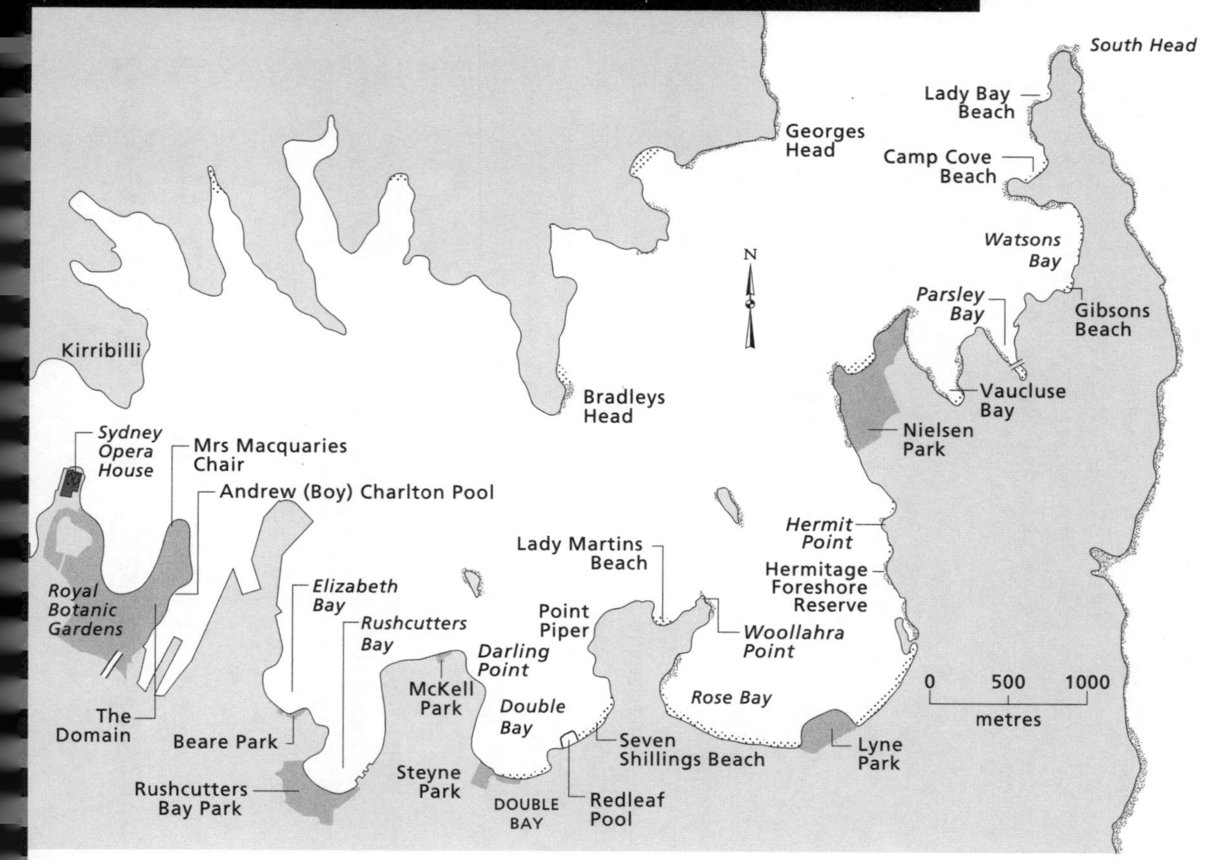
South Head
Lady Bay Beach
Georges Head
Camp Cove Beach
Watsons Bay
Parsley Bay
Gibsons Beach
N
Kirribilli
Vaucluse Bay
Bradleys Head
Nielsen Park
Sydney Opera House
Mrs Macquaries Chair
Andrew (Boy) Charlton Pool
Hermit Point
Lady Martins Beach
Hermitage Foreshore Reserve
Royal Botanic Gardens
Elizabeth Bay
Point Piper
Rushcutters Bay
Woollahra Point
Darling Point
0 500 1000
metres
Rose Bay
McKell Park
Double Bay
The Domain
Beare Park
Seven Shillings Beach
Lyne Park
Steyne Park
Rushcutters Bay Park
DOUBLE BAY
Redleaf Pool

Royal Botanic Gardens, Farm Cove, Sydney

Sydney's 30-hectare Royal Botanic Gardens sweep down to the water at Farm Cove east of the Sydney Opera House providing a glorious green retreat not far from the heart of the city's Central Business District. Officially established on 9 hectares of farm land as early as 1816, the gardens are now home to more than 7500 plants from all over the world. They are open 7 days from sunrise (7 am to 8 am) to sunset (between 5 pm and 8 pm), depending on the time of year. **Walkers** (and joggers) make good use of the well-maintained paths along the sea wall and throughout the gardens and there are free guided walks that are most informative. Riding bicycles is prohibited, but a trackless train provides an effortless ride to view some of the attractions. Plenty of **shade** and **seating** and charming secluded spots for private **picnics**.

For further information, check out the Visitor Centre near the entrance from Mrs Macquaries Road, open 7 days from 9.30 am to 4.30 pm, phone 9231 8125.

Of special interest is the **Tropical Centre**, comprised of the Pyramid Glasshouse and The Ark, open 10 am to 4 pm, the **Palm Grove** and the **Rose Garden**. During the Festival of Sydney, in January and February each year, the gardens and nearby Domain are the scene of some popular outdoor events.

Ferry: *to Circular Quay, less than a kilometre away.*
Bus: *any of the many buses to Circular Quay; Elizabeth Street buses.*
Train: *to Circular Quay, less than a kilometre away.*
Car: *access from Mrs Macquaries Road or Macquarie Street, Sydney.*
Water taxi: *to Opera House jetty.*
Amenities: *park, parking, seating, shade, toilets, views, walking, wheelchair access.*

Architectural majesty—the classic vista of the Opera House at sunset.

The Domain—a peaceful retreat from the hustle and bustle of the city.

Mrs Macquarie's Chair—spectacular harbour views can be seen from here.

HMAS *Sydney's* prow, Garden Island.

Clarke Island, off Darling Point.

Rushcutters Bay, home of the Crusing Yacht Club.

A fine stone residence sits elegantly beside the water at Double Bay.

Vaucluse House, located on Vaucluse Reserve, is a beautiful old home and a natural heritage site, which is open to the public.

Above: Seaplanes provide alternative modes of transport around the harbour.
Below: Point Piper divides Rose Bay and Double Bay.

Shark nets keep swimming safe at Neilsen Park.

Dover Heights in the eastern suburbs commands breathtaking harbour views.

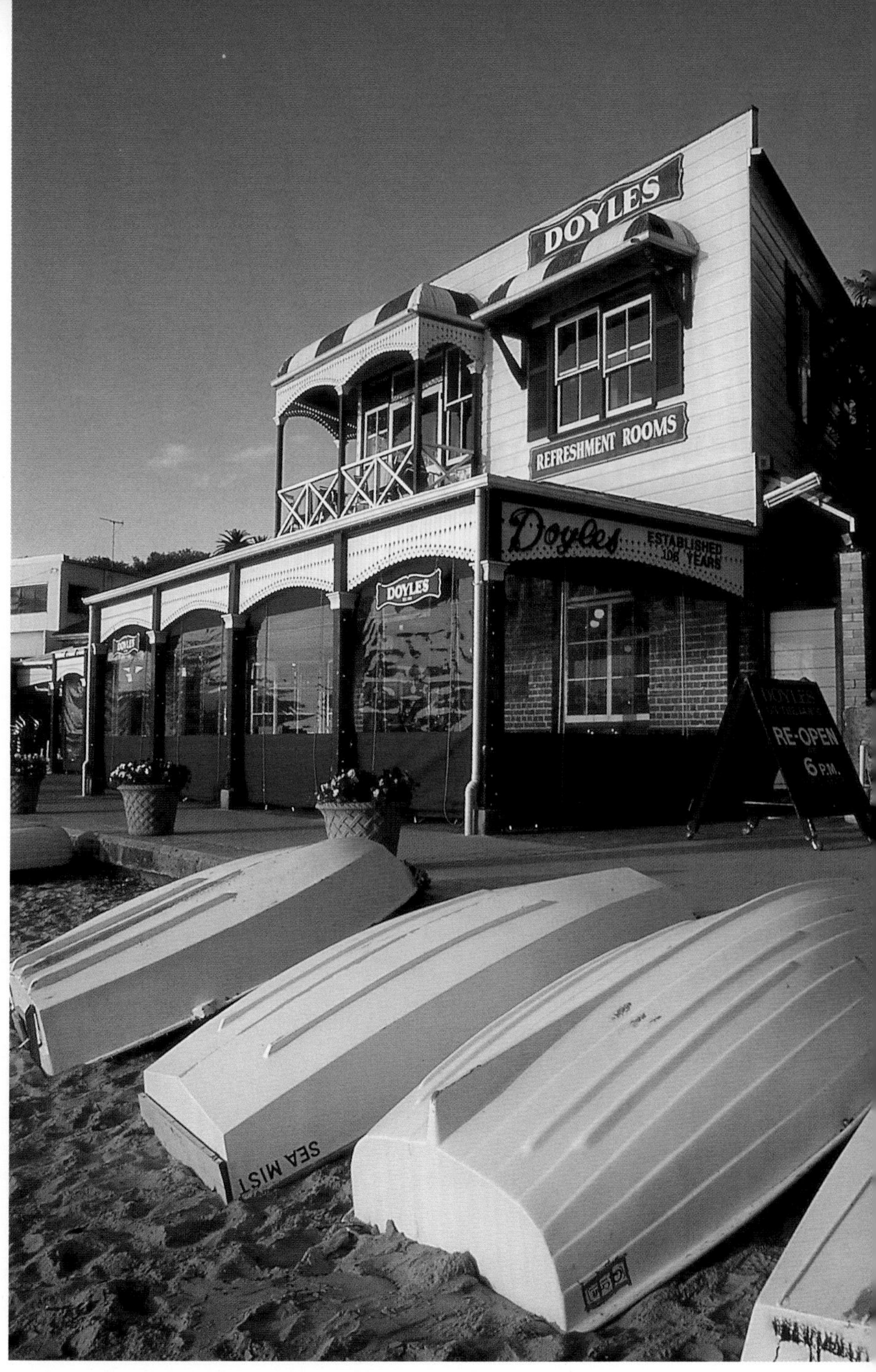

Doyle’s original restaurant at Watsons Bay is a Sydney institution.

A spectacular aerial vista, looking south from South Head.

Mrs Macquaries Chair, The Domain, Sydney

Top Spot

The Domain is a vast expanse of interrupted **parkland** extending from St Mary's Cathedral in the heart of the city to Mrs Maquaries Point at the end of the peninsula between Wolloomoloo Bay and Farm Cove. Mrs Macquarie, wife of an early governor, used to sit at a particular spot near the point to take the harbour air. The peninsula itself is quite commonly referred to as Mrs Macquaries Chair.

The **views** of the North Shore, the Sydney Opera House, the city and the Harbour Bridge are spectacular from this elevated grassy headland, which is a favourite with lunchtime joggers and wedding parties. Here is one of the best spots to observe the busy life of the water as ferries, showboats, yachts, cruisers and giant cargo vessels slide past, reminding us that this is very much a working harbour. It is also an excellent vantage point for harbour events such as the fireworks on Australia Day and New Year's Eve.

The peninsula is dotted with magnificent old trees, many of them Moreton Bay figs, providing plenty of **shade**. There is some **seating** and lovely **picnic** spots (but no barbecues) and a **jetty** that is mostly used for ceremonial occasions. **Fishing** is popular from the harbour wall along the harbourside walkway leading through the Royal Botanic Gardens to the opera house. The Olympic-size Andrew (Boy) Charlton Pool, named after a famous Australian swimmer, lies on the eastern shore of the peninsula.

Street **parking** is plentiful, although demand is high. The area can be **accessed** by **bike** or **wheelchair**.

Ferry: *none.*
Bus: *no. 441; Sydney Explorer Service.*
Train: *none.*
Car: *access from Mrs Macquaries Road.*
Water taxi: *to jetty on western side of park.*
Amenities: *bike access, fishing, jetty, park, parking, picnicking, pool, seating, shade, toilets, views, walking, wheelchair access.*

Beare Park, Elizabeth Bay

This small but charming **park** located in a very high-density suburb is a pretty spot, worth a visit if you are in the area. It is flat, with a harbour wall, lots of small open grassy areas and enough trees for **shade**, especially a little back from the water. The park has one of a very few ornate metal Victorian drinking fountains still to be found in the Sydney area.

There are a couple of cute **picnic** areas with a children's **playground** and some pleasant **views** across the harbour. There is also a little **seating** and quite a bit of **shade** under some fine old trees. **Fishing** is popular here. There are also **toilets** and a **phone**.

While there is some street **parking**, this spot is probably most easily reached by car or bus. The park can be **accessed** by **wheelchair** but bikes are prohibited.

Ferry: *none.*
Bus: *along Billyard Avenue, no. 311.*
Train: *none.*
Car: *access from Ithaca Road.*
Water taxi: *none.*
Amenities: *parking, fishing, park, phone, picnicking, playground, seating, shade, toilets, views, wheelchair access.*

Rushcutters Bay Park, Rushcutters Bay

Top Spot This park is most famous for being the home base of the Cruising Yacht Club, which runs the classic Sydney–Hobart Yacht Race every Boxing Day. Together with Yarranabbe Park, which runs along the western shore of the Darling Point peninsula, Rushcutters Bay serves as the lungs of the Elizabeth Bay–Darling Point area.

One of the best amenities is the tennis centre and oval complex. Australian football, soccer, athletics and other sports are played on the oval and the tennis courts are rarely empty. Once a year the park goes cultural, when the Tropicana Short Film Festival overflows here from its base in nearby Darlinghurst.

Fishing is popular over the wall and from the **jetty**, and the park has ample room for jogging and plenty of private spots for **picnics**, and a **toilet** block. There is also a large and well-equipped children's **playground** and, hidden away behind the marinas, two delightful waterside cafes with outdoor tables from which you can watch boats being prepared for sailing.

All of which lies in sharp contrast to the park's bloody history—Rushcutters Bay was named after two rushcutters who were speared to death by local Aboriginal people in early colonial times.

There is a fair amount of street **parking** around the perimeter as well as **wheelchair** and **bike access.**

Ferry: *none.*
Bus: *along New South Head Road, nos 323–327.*
Train: *none.*
Car: *access from New Beach Road and Waratah Street.*
Water taxi: *to the marina.*
Amenities: *bike access, fishing, jetty, park, parking, picnicking, playground, seating, shade, toilets, views, walking, wheelchair access.*

McKell Park, Darling Point

Top Spot

Although quite small and steep, and not very well known, this is one of Sydney Harbour's beautiful surprises. Its terraced garden, featuring tiny squares, pathways and elegant plant-beds, tumbles down the end of Darling Point towards the water. Linked by several sets of stone steps, it has a strong Continental atmosphere, while the ruins of the colonial McKell House evoke the days of convicts, wool and rum and of the many sailing ships that docked where the ferry wharf now stands.

Recently expanded, the **park** now has a substantial harbour frontage, incorporating some fine **picnic** spots, lovely water vistas, and public **toilets**. It is large enough for an energetic stroll and the **views** are magnificent. There is **seating** and **shade** and a **jetty** to **fish** from.

There is no parking at all, so it is best to come here by ferry or bus, and **wheelchair access** is limited to the top section of the park. The park is open from 7 am to 7.30 pm.

Ferry: *to Darling Point Wharf.*
Bus: *along Darling Point Road, no. 327.*
Train: *none.*
Car: *access from Darling Point Road, Darling Point.*
Water taxi: *to Darling Point Wharf.*
Amenities: *fishing, jetty, park, picnicking, seating, shade, toilets, views, walking, wheelchair access (limited).*

Steyne Park, Double Bay

Just a short walk from Double Bay's stylish shops and cafes, this spacious open grassy **park**, also known as Double Bay Park, has a good range of amenities and a pleasant swimming **beach**, shielded from public view by a wall.

There is **seating**, **shade** and some **picnic tables**, along with a well-designed **playground**, **toilets**, a **phone**, and a **rotunda**. Adjacent to the beach and park, there is a **boat ramp** and the Eighteen Foot Sailing Club has a bar and restaurant overlooking the water.

Fishing is popular from the **jetty** or the beach and many people come here to enjoy a brisk **walk** at lunchtime, after work or on weekends. There is a **bike** path running behind the beach, and the park has plenty of space for ball games.

People in **wheelchairs** can enjoy all of this park because of the well-made paths and flat terrain. There is some street **parking** but being close to the ferry wharf, the demand is heavy.

Ferry: *to Bay Street Wharf.*
Bus: *to Double Bay, no. 330; along New South Head Road, nos 323–325, a few hundred metres away.*
Train: *none.*
Car: *access from Bay Street, Double Bay.*
Water taxi: *to ferry wharf.*
Amenities: *beach, bike access, boat ramp, fishing, jetty, park, parking, phone, picnic tables, playground, rotunda, seating, shade, toilets, views, walking, wheelchair access.*

Redleaf Pool and Seven Shillings Beach, Double Bay

Redleaf is a large and well-maintained enclosed harbour swimming pool situated at the bottom of a cliff behind Woollahra Council Chambers in New South Head Road. Also blessed with a lovely **beach** and modest **views** across the harbour, there is a pleasantly **shady** grassed area behind the sand. A high wooden walkway runs all around the **pool**, which is safe, patrolled and friendly.

The kiosk and cafe by the pool is certainly needed after clambering down the many steps from road level. There are also **change rooms**, **seating**, **toilets** and a **phone**. The council chambers behind the pool hire out function rooms, and poetry readings are held from time to time in Blackburn Gardens above the pool. **Parking** is limited and there is no wheelchair access, but a cyclist can park a bike easily enough.

Neighbouring Seven Shillings Beach can be accessed via a gate from the pool. It is a bare, quiet extension of the beach at Redleaf, without any amenities, and is also accessible by road from St Mervyns Avenue.

Ferry: *none.*
Bus: *along New South Head Road, nos 323–325.*
Train: *none.*
Car: *access from New South Head Road and St Mervyns Avenue.*
Water taxi: *to the pool jetty.*
Amenities: *beach, change rooms, function rooms, jetty, park, phone, pool, seating, shade, toilets, views, walking.*

Lady Martins Beach, Point Piper

Nestling between Point Piper and Woollahra Point, this small **beach** beside the Royal Prince Edward Yacht Club may have good **views** up the harbour but it offers very little in the way of amenities to the public, although **sailboards** can be launched from it.

Because of its relatively inaccessible location (tucked away off a cul de sac), the lack of parking and the fact that it is prone to collect rubbish floating in from the water, it is not recommended as a beach for visitors.

The beach is not accessible by bike or wheelchair.

Ferry: *none.*
Bus: *along New South Head Road, no. 325.*
Train: *none.*
Car: *access from Wolseley Road, Point Piper.*
Water taxi: *none.*
Amenities: *beach, sailboard access, views.*

Port Jackson Shark

First named in 1793 by Meyer, a scientist, this shark was at first thought to be unique to Sydney Harbour, but was later found to frequent most Australian coastal waters. A nocturnal bottom shark with few predators, it is rarely seen in the harbour, but specimens are occasionally tagged by scientists in order to study migration and distribution. They are thought to breed in shallow waters, possibly including the harbour, in July and August. Apparently they pose no threat to humans.

Lyne Park, Rose Bay

Flat and grassy with large Moreton Bay figs, low-lying Lyne Park spreads out into Rose Bay between two stretches of **beach**. The western 'beach' is more a length of sand below the long promenade curving around the bay and is totally submerged at high tide. The eastern beach is so shallow it is perfect for learning to sailboard, although not really suitable for swimming, and sand flats stretch out into the bay at low tide.

The **park** has a **boat ramp** next to the ferry wharf and several fine restaurants beside the water as well as one floating on it (see Facilities At A Glance; Restaurants and Cafes, page 168). There are **change rooms**, plenty of **seating** and **shade** and even several quiet little hideaway areas close to the water and under large old spreading trees, where you can get away from the crowds and **picnic**, talk or just meditate.

The park is large so there is more than enough room for quite an extensive **walk** along the shore, particularly if you begin at the city end of the promenade and make your way around the bay and through the park itself to the eastern beach. **Sailboards** and small boats can be hired at Tingara Reserve behind this beach, which is busy throughout the warmer months. To top it all off, there is an eight court-tennis complex (which is almost always full) and a large RSL club with restaurant, bistro and bar just behind the reserve.

An ample **carpark** is provided but public transport is plentiful. The park is **bike** and **wheelchair accessible**.

Ferry: *to Rose Bay Ferry Wharf.*
Bus: *along New South Head Road, nos 323–325.*
Train: *none.*
Car: *access from New South Head Road.*
Water taxi: *to the ferry wharf or the Lyne Park jetty.*
Amenities: *beach, bike access, boat ramp, carpark, change rooms, fishing, jetty, park, phone, picnicking, playground, sailboard access, seating, shade, toilets, views, walking, wheelchair access.*

Nielsen Park and Hermitage Foreshore Reserve, Vaucluse

Top Spot Now part of the Sydney Harbour National Park, Nielsen Park covers most of the headland between Vaucluse Bay and Rose Bay. The Hermitage Foreshore Reserve adjoins the **park** and follows the water's edge around Hermit Point to the Rose Bay Convent. Rocky foreshores with marvellous **views** up and down the harbour combine with tiny secluded **beaches**, dense bushland, grassy open areas, and **shady** fig trees to make this area one of Sydney Harbour's truly top spots.

Once part of the estate of pioneer explorer and politician, William Charles Wentworth, Nielsen Park today offers a beach—Shark Beach—netted in summer, and a restaurant, as well as plenty of **shade** and **seating**. This is one of the best places from which to view the start of the Sydney–Hobart Yacht Race on Boxing Day. There is enough room for quite an extensive **walk** on Hermitage Foreshore around to Rose Bay. It does have quite a few steps, so reasonable fitness is required.

There is an excellent **picnic** area, **change rooms**, **toilets**, a **phone** and function rooms in the superb Italian restaurant. **Fishing** is allowed in the area and **sailboards** may be launched from here. Greycliffe House, an 1870s mansion built by the Wentworth family, stands in the park and is open to the public on weekdays. **Access** by **bike** or **wheelchair** is possible—but not to the path along the Hermitage Foreshore.

Ferry: *none.*
Bus: *along Wentworth Road, no. 325.*
Train: *none.*
Car: *access from Greycliffe Avenue.*
Water taxi: *none.*
Amenities: *beach, bike access, change rooms, fishing, park, parking, phone, picnic area, pool (net up in summer only), sailboard access, seating, shade, toilets, views, walking, wheelchair access.*

Vaucluse Bay, Vaucluse

A large **park** with a small shallow protected **beach**, this is an ideal picnic area for families. There are few amenities but Vaucluse Park itself, which extends back across Wentworth Road into the gully around historic Vaucluse House, is grassy and open with bushy hillsides. At about two hectares, it is quite substantial in area—large enough for a stroll after lunch. Vaucluse House is open Tuesday to Sunday 10 am to 4.30 pm.

The park has some **shade**, as well as pleasant **picnic spots**, though no picnic tables and no real views to speak of. The beach is backed by a meadow of grass that comes right down to the sand in places and is dotted with trees. The creek that flows down to the beach is more of a stormwater drain and the water isn't always clean enough for swimming. **Sailboards** can be launched here.

This spot's main attraction, however, is Vaucluse House itself. This grand colonial mansion was the home of the explorer and statesman William Charles Wentworth. The house is open to the public, with every room set up as it would have been in Wentworth's day, and you can see the cells under the house where the convicts slept. The excellent tea rooms adjacent to the House sell lunch and afternoon teas.

There is an ample **carpark** for Vaucluse House and plenty of street **parking**, although it gets very congested on hot summer weekends. The area can be **accessed** by **wheelchair**.

Ferry: *none.*
Bus: *along Wentworth Road, no. 325; Bondi & Bay Explorer.*
Train: *none.*
Car: *access from Wentworth Road, Vaucluse.*
Water taxi: *none.*
Amenities: *beach, carpark, park, picnicking, sailboard access, seating, shade, toilets (at Vaucluse House), walking, wheelchair access.*

Parsley Bay, Vaucluse

This little known **park** and **beach**, much loved by the locals, is hidden in a small deep valley among the expensive houses of Vaucluse. A picturesque old footbridge across the valley high above the narrow stretch of water is a special feature of the bay.

The beach is netted against sharks and, while it is quite deep at the net where swimmers lap across the sheltered waters, the shallow beach end of the bay is often filled with children. The park is open and fairly flat with substantial grassy areas suitable for throwing frisbees and some good **picnic** spots. A pleasant feature is the fine old trees, including Moreton Bay figs, which provide large areas of **shade** a little back from the water.

There is also a small **playground**, **seating**—mostly under the trees—as well as a **kiosk**, **change rooms** and **toilets**. People often **fish** or sunbake just outside the net and take a gentle stroll from the park along the path beside the bay to the net, or up to the bridge, which is just enough to stretch the legs. There are no real views.

There is some **parking**, and the park is **accessible** by **bike**, although **wheelchair** access is limited.

Ferry: *none.*
Bus: *along nearby Fitzwilliam Road, no. 325.*
Train: *none.*
Car: *access from The Crescent or Horler Avenue, Vaucluse.*
Water taxi: *to the jetty.*
Amenities: *beach, bike access, change rooms, fishing, kiosk, park, parking, picnic areas, playground, seating, shade, toilets, walking, wheelchair access (limited).*

Watsons Bay

Top Spot This wide bay with several stretches of **beach** is a busy, popular area for sightseeing, dining, drinking and boating. The bay boasts excellent **views** towards the city skyline, a large **park** and lots of room for a harbourside stroll as well as fine restaurants and cafes. One of the big attractions is Doyle's Watsons Bay Hotel, with its huge beer garden overlooking the harbour. Doyle's on the Beach, a famous Sydney seafood restaurant, is on the pedestrian concourse that curves east around the bay.

Robertson Park, behind the bay, slopes gently up from the promenade, with a splendid avenue of palms as well as spreading Moreton Bay figs providing plenty of **shade** for cool **picnics** in summer. It contains a large and well-equipped children's **playground**, **picnic tables**, **toilets**, **seating** and a **rotunda**. Functions can be held at the Fishermens Lodge Restaurant, which is a historic house in the park.

The beach area is also well equipped, boasting an enclosed harbour swimming **pool**, a **phone** and **jetty**—a popular spot for **fishing**. **Sailboards** can be launched from any of the beaches. The swimming is not marvellous around the jetty area because of boat-oil pollution but just 100 metres south, half hidden by the Harbour Pilot's Station, Gibsons Beach is clean and relatively empty.

Watsons Bay has a large **parking** area, crowded on weekends, and there is **bike** and **wheelchair access**.

Ferry: *to Fishermans Wharf, Watsons Bay.*
Bus: *to Watsons Bay, nos 324, 325 & L82.*
Train: *none.*
Car: *access from Military Road, Watsons Bay.*
Water taxi: *to Watsons Bay Wharf.*
Amenities: *beach, bike access, fishing, jetty, park, parking, phone, picnic tables, playground, pool, rotunda, sailboard access, seating, shade, toilets, views, walking, wheelchair access.*

Camp Cove Beach, Watsons Bay

Top Spot

Camp Cove **beach** is distinguished by its unusually yellow crescent of sand, which slips quite quickly into deep green waters. At night it can be magical, with phosphorescence glistening in the waves. So-named because Captain Phillip camped here with a party of men on his first expedition into Sydney Harbour, today the beach plays host to leathery skinned regulars, international tourists, scuba divers and 'beautiful people'.

At the south end of the beach the elevated hump of grassy Green Point Reserve overlooks the cove as well as offering magnificent **views** up and down the harbour. Here you can **picnic** and enjoy the vistas from the **shade** of huge trees. At the northern end, wooden steps lead up to the path, which follows the foreshore past Lady Bay Beach to the end of South Head, part of the Sydney Harbour National Park.

Camp Cove itself has **toilets** and a well-equipped **kiosk**. People **fish** from the rocks, snorkel and scuba dive and **sailboards** may be launched from here. The beach is **accessible** by **wheelchair** at the northern end only. Camp Cove has a spacious but usually crowded **parking** area, and street parking is limited, so public transport is probably a good idea.

Ferry: *to Fishermans Wharf, Watsons Bay, less than a kilometre away.*
Bus: *to Watsons Bay, nos 324, 325 & L82.*
Train: *none.*
Car: *access from Pacific or Cliff streets, Watsons Bay.*
Water taxi: *to Watsons Bay Wharf, less than a kilometre away.*
Amenities: *beach, beach shower, bike access, carpark, fishing, kiosk, park, picnicking, sailboard access, shade, toilets, views, walking, wheelchair access (limited).*

Lady Bay Beach, South Head

One of Sydney's few nude **beaches**, this small and pleasant stretch of sand backed by a high curve of cliff wall and scrub is the last beach on the South Head peninsula before the harbour opens out to the ocean. The **views** from this spot across the harbour to Middle Head are spectacular.

The beach is reached by fairly steep steps (so make sure you are reasonably fit) and there are **toilets** near the top of them. The steps descend from the **walking** track that runs through this part of Sydney Harbour National Park from Camp Cove to the tip of South Head. There are no amenities here at all—just a beautiful, secluded strip of sand, still with a harbour character but close to the ocean, and visited by what feels like the freshest and cleanest sea breeze you will get anywhere in Sydney.

The beach is fringed at either end by rocks and scrub, often dotted with people sunbathing. There is a little taste of the world's turbulent history here, in the shape of some colonial-era gun emplacements set into the cliffs above the beach.

The nearest **parking** area is at Camp Cove, about one kilometre away, though that fills up very early in the morning. There is no bike or wheelchair access.

Ferry: *to Watsons Bay, around two kilometres away.*
Bus: *to Watsons Bay, nos 324 & 325, two kilometres away.*
Train: *none.*
Car: *access from Cliff Street, Watsons Bay, less than a kilometre away.*
Water taxi: *to Watsons Bay.*
Amenities: *beach, toilets, views, walking.*

South Head, Watsons Bay

To stand on South Head is to command one of the most magnificent **views**, with almost 360° vistas of harbour and city, across to North Head and Middle Head and out to sea.

South Head is just a high, bare, bushy promontory, with Hornby Lighthouse and the lighthouse keeper's cottage evoking images of tall ships entering the harbour during the early days of the colony. There are also old concrete bunkers from this century's wars.

Many have enjoyed the harbour since those historic times, as will many more to come. So it is fitting that we end both this book and this adventure here.

Ferry: *to Watsons Bay, about two-and-a-half kilometres away.*
Bus: *to Watsons Bay, nos 324 & 325, about two-and-a-half kilometres away.*
Train: *none.*
Car: *access from Cliff Street, Watsons Bay, about one-and-a-half kilometres away.*
Water taxi: *to Watsons Bay.*
Amenities: *fabulous views.*

Facilities at a Glance

This section allows you both to fast-track and focus on your own particular interests in Sydney Harbour. For example, if you want to hire a boat, look up Boating. Then look up the main listings section to decide which part of the harbour you would like to visit.

If you are looking for a quiet, out-of-the-way spot for, say, a picnic, look up Hideaways, then turn to the main listings to learn more about the hideaway that most appeals to you.

So start perusing the Facilities at a Glance section and good luck with your visit to Sydney Harbour.

BEACHES

Northern Harbour

Athol Bay beach Mosman. Access from Athol Wharf Road, page 58.
Balmoral Beach Mosman. Access from The Esplanade, page 44.
Blues Point Reserve McMahons Point. Access from Blues Point Road, page 76.
Bonds Reserve Greenwich. Access from O'Connell Street, page 83.
Castle Rock Beach Balgowlah. Access from Ogilvy Road, page 35.
Chinamans Beach The Spit. Access from McLean Street, page 43.
Clarkes Point Beach Woolwich. Access from Woolwich Road, page 86.
Clifton Gardens Beach Mosman. Access from Morella Road, page 55.
Clontarf Beach Clontarf. Access from Holmes Avenue, page 36.
Cobblers Beach Middle Head, Georges Heights. Access from Middle Head Road, page 45.
Collins Beach Sydney Harbour National Park, North Head, Manly. Access from Stuart Street, Manly, page 18.
Delwood Beach Manly. Access from Commonwealth Parade, page 27.
East Esplanade beach Manly. Access from East Esplanade, page 21.
Fairlight Beach Fairlight. Access from Lauderdale Avenue, page 28.
Forty Baskets Beach Balgowlah. Access from Beatty Street, page 31.
Greenwich Baths Greenwich. Access from Albert Street, page 84.
Lavender Bay North Sydney. Access from Harbour View Crescent, page 75.
Little Manly Point Park beach Manly. Access from Stuart Street, page 19.
Little Sirius Cove beach Mosman. Access from Sirius Cove Road, page 60.
Neutral Bay Wharf beach Neutral Bay. Access from Hayes Street, page 65.
Obelisk Bay beach Middle Head, Georges Heights. Access from Chowder Bay Road, page 46.
Reef Beach Balgowlah. Access from Beatty Street, page 33.
Sandy Bay beach Clontarf. Access from Sandy Bay Road, page 37.
Taylors Bay beach Mosman. Access from Iluka Road, page 56.
The Spit beach Access from Spit Road, page 40.
Waverton Park beach Waverton. Access from Woolcott Street, page 78.
West Esplanade beach Manly. Access from West Esplanade, page 25.

Whiting Beach Mosman. Access via walking track from Whiting Beach Road or from Athol Wharf, Athol Wharf Road, page 59.

Southern Harbour

Camp Cove beach Watsons Bay. Access from Pacific Street and Cliff Street, page 147.

'Colgate-Palmolive' beach Balmain East. Access from Duke Street, page 108.

Double Bay beach Double Bay. Access from Bay Street, page 139.

Elkington Park Balmain. Access from Glassop Street, page 104.

Gibsons Beach Watsons Bay. Access from Marine Parade, page 146.

Hermit Bay beach Vaucluse. Access from Carrara Road, page 178.

Hermit Point beach Vaucluse. Access from Little Queens Avenue, page 143.

Lady Bay Beach Watsons Bay. Access via walking track past Camp Cove from Cliff Street, Watsons Bay, page 148.

Lady Martins Beach Point Piper. Access from Wolseley Road, page 141.

Lyne Park beach Rose Bay. Access from New South Head Road, page 142.

Milk Beach Vaucluse. Access from Carrara Road, page 178.

Parsley Bay beach Vaucluse. Access from Parsley Road and The Crescent, page 145.

Seven Shillings Beach Double Bay. Access via Blackburn Gardens off New South Head Road, page 140.

Shark (Nielsen Park) Beach Vaucluse. Access from Greycliffe Avenue, page 143.

Vaucluse Bay beach Vaucluse. Access from Wentworth Road, page 144.

Watsons Bay beach Watsons Bay. Access from Military Road, page 146

BOATING

(See also Boat Launch Ramps)

Boat users on Sydney Harbour should acquaint themselves with all safety and licensing regulations.

BOAT HIRE

This list is not exhaustive. New companies form and old ones close down. Most marinas have some boats for hire.

Admiral Charters Waverton. Phone: 9955 9961.

Board-a-Boat Sydney. Phone: 9267 3610.

Eastsail Rushcutters Bay.
Phone: 9327 1166.
Elizabeth Bay Marina Elizabeth Bay.
Phone: 9358 2057.
Rose Bay Marina Rose Bay.
Phone: 9363 5930.
Sail Australia Mosman.
Phone: 9960 6111.
Sydney Ferries Phone: 131 500.

Alcohol and Water Do Not Mix

This message, emphasised by the Waterways Authority, cannot be too strongly stressed. A disproportionate number of accidents on Sydney Harbour are caused by alcohol. You are required to remain under 0.05% blood alcohol level on the water, just as you are behind the wheel of a car.

Buying Second-hand Boats

To avoid being cheated when you buy a second-hand boat, call REVs (the Register of Encumbered Vehicles), a free service provided by the Department of Fair Trading. They will inform you whether the boat you are intending to buy has money owing on it and may be repossessed without compensation to you.
Phone: 9600 0022.

Charters

The Charter Boat Information Service will find a boat, large or small, to fit your charter requirements.
Phone: 9552 1827.

Ice-cream Boat

This boat cruises the harbour, selling ice-creams, drinks and snacks. They have a 'round' that takes them to all the beaches and fishing areas so watch out for them, although, as you would expect, their prices are significantly higher than shop prices.

JET SKIING

These small jet-driven watercraft, ridden like a motorbike, are not permitted in many areas of the harbour. A licence is required to drive these vehicles and there are regulations regarding size and performance. Check with the Waterways Authority for details.
Phone: 9563 8511 or 13 12 56.

SAILBOARDING

Sailboarding is restricted to certain areas in Sydney Harbour. It is permitted along the North Shore in bays east of Kirribilli including all of Middle Harbour and parts of North Harbour and Manly Cove; anywhere west of Yurulbin (previously Long Nose) Point, Birchgrove, and Manns Point, Greenwich; and in Eastern Suburbs bays to the tip of South Head.

It is forbidden in the main shipping channels down the length of the centre of the harbour to Manly and out the heads, including anywhere from Yurulbin (previously Long Nose) Point, Birchgrove, and Manns Point, Greenwich, to Careening Cove, Kirribilli, on the North Shore and Elizabeth Bay on the south side of the harbour.

Contact the Waterways Authority on 9563 8511 for a map detailing prohibited areas.

BOAT LAUNCH RAMPS

While public boat ramps are fairly scarce, some marinas may, by agreement, allow boats to be launched.

Northern Harbour

Balmoral Beach Mosman. Access from The Esplanade.
Bonds Reserve Greenwich. Access from O'Connell Street.
Careening Cove Kirribilli. Access from McDougall Street.
Clarkes Point Woolwich. Access from Clarke Road.
Clontarf Reserve Clontarf. Access from Monash Crescent.
Greenwich Wharf Greenwich (very small boats only). Access from Mitchell Street.
Kellys Bush Reserve Woolwich. Foot of Margaret Street.
Kirribilli Access from Kirribilli Avenue, Kirribilli.
Lavender Bay North Sydney. Access from Bay View Street.
Little Manly Cove Manly. Access from Craig Avenue.
Manns Point Greenwich. Access from Prospect Street.

Southern Harbour

Bicentennial Park Glebe. Access from The Crescent, Glebe.
Lyne Park Rose Bay. Access from New South Head Road.
Steyne Park Double Bay. Access from Bay Street.
Watsons Bay beach. Access from Marine Parade.

BUSES

Bus route numbers and the streets at which to alight are included for readers' convenience. While correct at the time of writing, bus route numbers listed in this book could change. To obtain accurate, current information about bus routes, route numbers, city departure points, alighting points and timetables, visitors should ring the Bus, Train and Ferry Information Line: **13 15 00**.

Sydney Buses also produces a range of leaflets and brochures clearly outlining all relevant information about bus services.

CLUBS

The law relating to clubs holds that only people residing within five kilometres may be members but anyone may be signed in as the guest of a member. The extent to which individual clubs abide by the law varies. So, if you wish to drink, eat or socialise at a club, it is wise to phone first and ascertain the conditions under which you may do so.

Northern Harbour

Australian Sailing School and Club Access from Spit Road, The Spit. Phone: 9960 3077.

Balmoral Sailing Club Access from The Esplanade, Mosman. Phone: 9969 8782.

Drummoyne Sailing Club 2 St Georges Crescent, Drummoyne. Phone: 9719 8199.

Greenwich Flying Squadron Access from Bay Street, Greenwich. Phone: 9436 1901.

Hunters Hill Sailing Club Access from Merrington Place, Woolwich. Phone: 9816 5319.

Manly 16ft Skiff Sailing Club Access from East Esplanade, Manly. Phone: 9977 3322.

Manly Yacht Club Access from East Esplanade, Manly. Phone: 9977 4949.

Middle Harbour 16ft Skiff Club Access from Spit Road, The Spit. Phone: 9960 1621.

Middle Harbour Yacht Club Access from Spit Road, The Spit. Phone: 9969 1244.

Mosman Rowing Club Access from Avenue Road, Mosman Bay, Mosman. Phone: 9953 7966.

Royal Sydney Yacht Squadron 33 Peel Street, Kirribilli. Phone: 9955 7171.

Sydney Flying Squadron
76 McDougall Street, Milsons Point. Phone: 9955 8350.

Southern Harbour

Cruising Yacht Club Access from New Beach Road, Darling Point. Phone: 9363 9731.
Double Bay Sailing Club Access from Bay Street, Double Bay. Phone: 9363 5577.
Eighteen Foot Sailing Club 77 Bay Street, Double Bay. Phone: 9363 2995.
Rose Bay RSL Club New South Head Road cnr Vickery Avenue, Rose Bay. Phone: 9371 9412.
Royal Motor Yacht Club 21 Wunulla Street, Point Piper. Phone: 9327 6828.
Royal Prince Edward Yacht Club Access from Wolseley Road, Point Piper. Phone: 9327 3149.
Woollahra Sailing Club Access from Vickery Avenue, Rose Bay. Phone: 9371 9805.

CONFERENCE AND CATERING VENUES

Many restaurants that aren't listed here will make rooms available for conferences or catered functions (see Restaurants, on page 167). Many cruise companies hire out boats for conferences or catered functions (see Cruises, on page 158, and Tours And Museums, on page 170).

Park Weddings
Outdoor weddings can be held on any park or reserve by negotiation with the relevant local council or the National Parks and Wildlife Service.

Northern Harbour

Athol House Function Centre Access from Bradleys Head Road, Mosman. Phone: 9968 4441.
Birkenhead Point Shopping Centre Access from Roseby Street/ Cary Street, Birkenhead Point. Phone: 9181 3922.
Clonny's Restaurant Access from Sandy Bay Road, Clontarf. Phone: 9948 2373.
Drummoyne Sailing Club 2 St Georges Crescent, Drummoyne. Phone: 9181 1421.
Ensemble Theatre 78 McDougall Street, Kirribilli. Phone: 9929 8877.
Middle Harbour 16ft Skiff Club 77 Parriwi Road, The Spit. Phone: 9960 1621.

Mosman Rowing Club Access from Avenue Road, Mosman. Phone: 9953 7966.

Oceanworld Access from West Esplanade, Manly. Phone: 9949 2644.

Old Quarantine Station Access from North Head Scenic Drive, Manly. Phone: 9977 6229.

Royal Sydney Yacht Squadron 33 Peel Street, Kirribilli. Phone: 9955 7171.

Sails Harbourside Restaurant 2 Henry Lawson Avenue, McMahons Point. Phone: 9955 5793.

Taronga Zoo Conference Centre Access from Bradleys Head Road, Mosman. Phone: 9969 2400.

Southern Harbour

Australian National Maritime Museum Access from Darling Drive, Darling Harbour, Sydney. Phone: 9552 7777.

Cruising Yacht Club Access from New Beach Road, Darling Point. Phone: 9363 9731.

Darling Harbour restaurants Access from Darling Drive, Darling Harbour, Sydney. Phone: 9286 0100 (Darling Harbour Authority; for some individual restaurants see Restaurants section).

IMAX Theatre Access from Darling Drive, Darling Harbour, Sydney. Phone: 9281 3300.

Eighteen Foot Sailing Club 77 Bay Street, Double Bay. Phone: 9363 2995.

Fishermans Lodge Restaurant 9 Marine Parade, Watsons Bay. Phone: 9337 1226.

Park Hyatt 7 Hickson Road, The Rocks. Phone: 9241 1234.

Rodd Island Access by boat, Sydney Harbour National Park, Iron Cove. Phone: 9247 5033 (Sydney Harbour Information Centre).

Royal Botanic Gardens Restaurant Access from Mrs Macquaries Road, Sydney. Phone: 9231 8111.

Rose Bay RSL Club New South Head Road cnr Vickery Avenue, Rose Bay. Phone: 9371 9412.

South Steyne (permanently moored old Manly ferry). Access from Darling Drive, Darling Harbour, Sydney. Phone: 9211 5999.

Star City Casino 80 Pyrmont Street, Pyrmont. Phone: 9777 9000.

Sydney Convention Centre Access from Darling Drive, Darling Harbour. Phone: 9282 5000.

Sydney Ferries hire boats Phone: 13 15 00.

Sydney Fish Market Access from Pyrmont Bridge Road, Pyrmont. Phone: 9660 1611.

Sydney Opera House Access from Macquarie Street, Sydney. Phone: 9250 7111.

Sydney Theatre Company
Pier 4, Hickson Road, Dawes Point.
Phone: 9250 1700.
Watersedge Restaurant Pier One, Hickson Road, Millers Point.
Phone: 9247 4927.
Watsons Bay Hotel 1 Military Road, Watsons Bay. Phone: 9337 4299.
Woollahra Municipal Chambers
536 New South Head Road, Double Bay. Phone: 9391 7000.

COUNCILS

(HARBOURSIDE)

Drummoyne 9819 6555
Hunters Hill 9816 1555
Lane Cove 9911 3555
Leichhardt 9367 9222
Manly 9976 1500
Mosman 9978 4000
North Sydney 9936 8100
Sydney 9265 9333
Woollahra 9391 7000

CRUISES

Helicopter and water taxi companies are included in this section.
Accor Cruises Offers dinner cruises. Phone: 9552 3904.
ATS Booking Services Will book any cruises, water taxis or boat hires for you. Phone: 9555 2700.
Captain Cook Cruises Is a large company with many cruise craft ranging in size from small cruisers up to near liners. Daily departures. Phone: 9206 1111.
Ferries See Sydney Ferries.
Flagship Charters Offers corporate entertaining and conferences afloat as well as yacht and speedboat hire. Phone: 9555 5901.
Grande Gondola Offers gondola cruises on Pyrmont Bay.
Phone: 9560 0737.
Harbour Taxi Boats Taxis also for hire for tailor-made cruises, water taxi 'limousine' available for that special occasion. Phone: 9555 1155.
Heli-Aust Offers helicopter cruises over the harbour. Phone: 9317 3402.
Luxury Yachting Offers dinner and luncheon cruises for small or large groups. Phone: 9371 0135.
Matilda and Sail Centre Cruises
Operates regular routes between the Sydney Opera House, Circular Quay and Darling Harbour.
Phone: 9264 7377. For more information, call the Darling Harbour infoline on 1902 260 568 or visit the Information Office next to Sega World, Darling Harbour.
Meridian Charter Company
Offers cruises on the yacht Kalypso.
Phone: 9555 1155.

Quayside Charters Has large and small corporate and recreational cruisers for hire. Phone: 9555 2600.
Sail Venture Cruises Offers daily cruises. Phone: 9262 3595.
Sydney Ferries Hire their craft and also run cruises. Phone: 13 15 00.
Sydney Harbour Water Taxis Taxis also for hire for tailor-made cruises. Phone: 9755 4660.
Sydney Helicopters Offers helicopter cruises. Phone: 9637 4455.
Sydney Showboats Offer dinner, cabaret and sightseeing cruises on paddlewheelers. Phone: 9552 2722.
Taxis Afloat Taxis also for hire for tailor-made cruises. Phone: 9955 3222.
The Bounty A floating restaurant in a replica of Captain Bligh's Bounty. Daily departures. Phone: 9247 1789.
Vagabond Cruises Half- or full-day cruises of harbour sights. Phone: 9660 0388.

DOGS

All harbourside local councils have indicated changes to be made in their policies regarding dogs because a new law, the Companion Animals Act, came into force on 1 July 1999. Therefore, the authors have decided not to include any references to dogs or how they are tolerated by individual councils except to indicate where they are expressly forbidden (in all national parks, for example). For information about current council policies, readers are advised to call councils direct (see Councils, on page 158, for contact numbers). For information about the new Act, contact State Parliament, phone: 9230 2111.

FERRIES

Details of ferry services may change, so to be certain of accurate, current information, call the Bus, Train and Ferry Information Line: **13 15 00** for information about fares, departure points, departure times, routes and route names. For information on what is available at your chosen destination, consult the list below and refer to the pages cited.

Northern Harbour

Cremorne Point Access from Milson Road.
Greenwich Access from Mitchell Street.
Kirribilli Access from Holbrook Avenue.

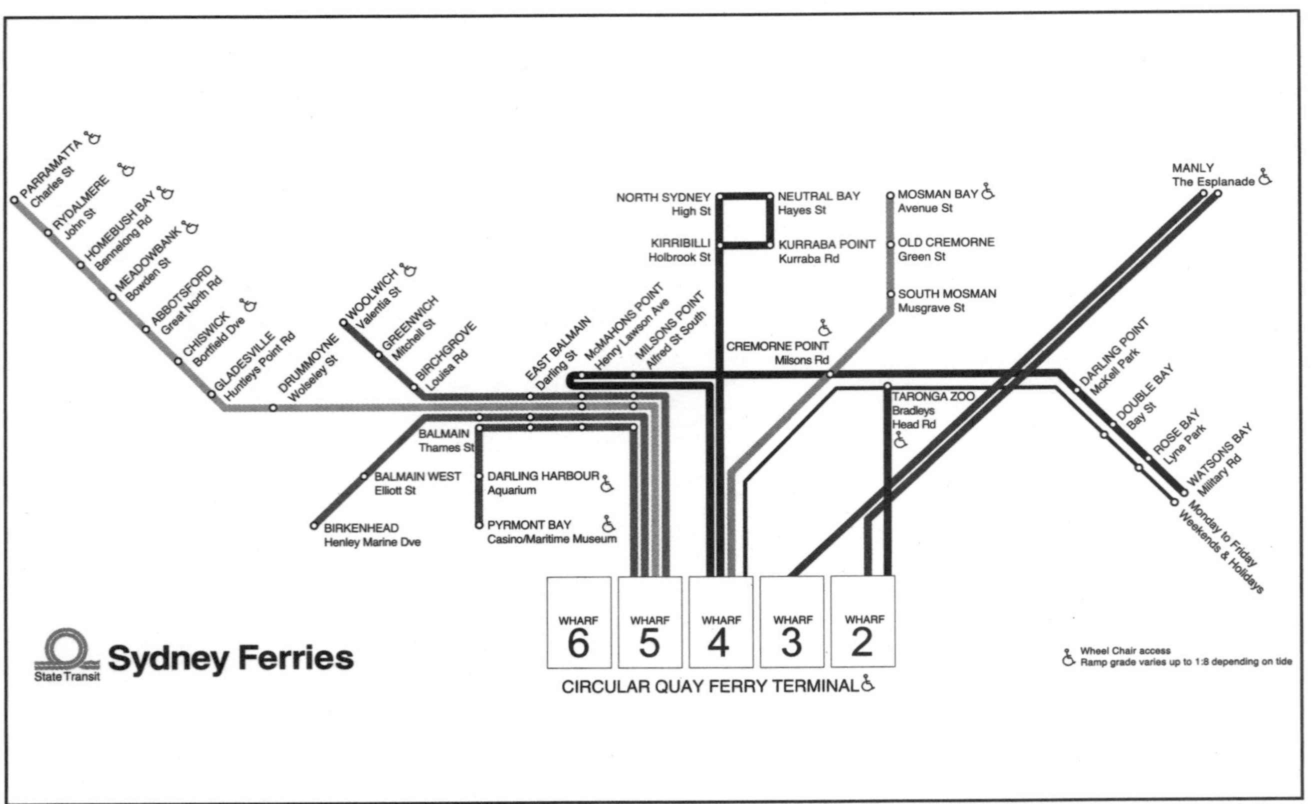
PARRAMATTA
Charles St
RYDALMERE
John St
HOMEBUSH BAY
Bennelong Rd
MEADOWBANK
Bowden St
ABBOTSFORD
Great North Rd
CHISWICK
Bortfield Dve
GLADESVILLE
Huntleys Point Rd
DRUMMOYNE
Wolseley St
WOOLWICH
Valentia St
GREENWICH
Mitchell St
BIRCHGROVE
Louisa Rd
EAST BALMAIN
Darling St
McMAHONS POINT
Henry Lawson Ave
MILSONS POINT
Alfred St South
NORTH SYDNEY
High St
KIRRIBILLI
Holbrook St
NEUTRAL BAY
Hayes St
KURRABA POINT
Kurraba Rd
CREMORNE POINT
Milsons Rd
MOSMAN BAY
Avenue St
OLD CREMORNE
Green St
SOUTH MOSMAN
Musgrave St
MANLY
The Esplanade
DARLING POINT
McKell Park
DOUBLE BAY
Bay St
ROSE BAY
Lyne Park
WATSONS BAY
Military Rd
Monday to Friday
Weekends & Holidays
TARONGA ZOO
Bradleys
Head Rd
BALMAIN
Thames St
BALMAIN WEST
Elliott St
BIRKENHEAD
Henley Marine Dve
DARLING HARBOUR
Aquarium
PYRMONT BAY
Casino/Maritime Museum
WHARF 6
WHARF 5
WHARF 4
WHARF 3
WHARF 2
CIRCULAR QUAY FERRY TERMINAL
State Transit
Sydney Ferries
Wheel Chair access
Ramp grade varies up to 1:8 depending on tide

Kurraba Point Access from Kurraba Road.
Manly Access from The Esplanade, Manly.
McMahons Point Access from Henry Lawson Avenue.
Milsons Point. Access from Alfred street South.
Mosman Access from Avenue Road.
Mosman South Access from Musgrove Street.
Neutral Bay Access from Hayes Street.
North Sydney Access from High Street.
Old Cremorne Access from Green Street.
Taronga Zoo Access from Bradleys Head Road.
Woolwich Access from Valentine Street.

Southern Harbour

Balmain Access from Thames Street.
Balmain East Access from Darling Street.
Balmain West Access from Elliott Street.
Birchgrove Access from Louisa Road.
Birkenhead Point Access from Henley Marine Drive.
Circular Quay Access from Alfred Street.
Darling Harbour Access near Sydney Aquarium.
Darling Point Access from Darling Point Road.
Double Bay Access from Bay Street.
Drummoyne Access from Wolseley Street.
Rose Bay Access from Lyne Park off New South Head Road.
Watsons Bay Access from Military Road.

FESTIVALS AND EVENTS

Summer

DECEMBER

Christmas Eve Carols on the Harbour at Darling Harbour. Phone: 9286 0111.
Boxing Day (the day after Christmas Day) Thousands of people line the harbour to watch the start of the **Sydney–Hobart Yacht Race**. Hundreds of spectator craft surging through the water are almost as spectacular as the billowing spinnakers of the yachts themselves. For all enquiries including where to find a good vantage point, contact the Cruising Yacht Club.
Phone: 9363 9731.
New Year's Eve Each New Year's Eve a spectacular fireworks display is

staged on and around the Sydney Harbour Bridge and Darling Harbour, sometimes even using buildings in the city. Find a spot early for a good view. For details contact the Darling Harbour Authority.
Phone: 9286 0100.

JANUARY

2–26: The Festival of Sydney runs through most of January and includes everything from outdoor street theatre to high art with some events on or near the harbour.
The Festival de Cuba at Darling Harbour runs from Thursday to Saturday from 8.15 pm for the duration of the festival. For details contact the Festival office.
Phone: 8248 6500.
26: The Australia Day Coca-Cola Amatil Ferry Boat Race churns down the harbour from Circular Quay toward the heads and back again to a finish line under the Sydney Harbour Bridge. Contact the Festival of Sydney for details.
Phone: 8248 6500.
The Australia Day Regatta is a popular yachting event that takes place at various locations around the harbour from 1.30 pm.
The Australia Day Fireworks Display is a spectacular free show for all the family, on at Darling Harbour from 9 pm. Darling Harbour also offers outdoor entertainment all day, including concerts, street theatre and an aquatic program.

JANUARY/FEBRUARY

Shakespeare Festival over eight weeks, Friday, Saturday and Sunday evenings. Balmoral Beach, Balmoral.
Phone: 9557 3065.

Autumn

MARCH

The Sydney Opera House Festival of Culture Dates vary from year to year. Phone: 9250 7111.
Greek National Day celebrations take place at the Sydney Opera House. Dates vary from year to year.
Phone: 9250 7111.
The Mosman Festival takes place on Balmoral Beach during the last weekend of March.
Phone: 9960 3196.
One night in March the **Tropicana Short Film Festival** spills over from Kings Cross into Rushcutters Bay Park—again, dates vary year from year to year. Phone: 9368 0434.
The Circus and Street Festival enlivens already lively Darling Harbour and runs throughout autumn. Phone: 9286 0100.

MAY

3: The "Mudgee" Food and Wine Festival at Balmoral Beach, Balmoral. Phone: (02) 6372 5875.

Winter

The Darling Harbour Jazz Festival Partly traditional, partly mainstream, always fun—not just for jazz lovers. Phone: 9286 0100.

Spring

A **spring multicultural festival** takes place at Darling Harbour every year and includes spectacular dragon-boat races. Phone: 9286 0100.

Throughout the year

The Sydney Opera House hosts outdoor markets on Sundays from 10 am to 5 pm and also offers music on the forecourt. Phone: 9250 7111.

Woollahra Municipal Chambers, Double Bay, offers occasional poetry readings. Phone: 9391 7000.

Contact the Sydney Organising Committee for the Olympic Games to find out which Olympic water events will take place on the harbour in 2000 and where. Phone: 9297 2000.

FISHING

What anglers most want to know is: what fish can I catch and where can I catch them? After extensive research, the answers to such questions are as elusive as the fish. In general, however, the following applies:

- The most common fish caught in most areas of the harbour are: bream, trevally, mulloway, snapper, dhufish, tailer, whiting, drummer, leatherjacket, blackfish and morwong. Near the entrance to the harbour you may also catch: lobster, kingfish, striped tuna, John Dory and other sea fishes.
- On an outgoing tide you are more likely to find flathead; on an incoming tide you are more likely to find bream, or so it is said. It may just be a fisherman's tale.
- In winter, you may be less likely to catch dhufish. In general, summer is better for fishing as in warmer waters fish tend to stay closer to the surface, whereas in the cold of winter they tend to remain in deeper waters.
- In all areas, fishing is best early or late in the day, as fish tend to head for deeper water during the middle of the day.

For best results, anyone interested in fishing on the harbour should consult any of the many excellent books available. One of the most popular of these is the New South Wales Fishing Atlas (see Further Reading, page 179, for details). This book, like others, lists the best spots in the harbour to catch particular fish, whether from the shore or from boats. The Great Outdoors Tide Guide, available at sports shops, newsagencies and some service stations can also be helpful (see Further Reading, page 179, for details).

To find out about the rules regarding fishing, there are two authorities. They are NSW Fisheries and the Waterways Authority. Fisheries concerns itself mostly with the water and the fish—the legal limits, excluded areas and so forth. Waterways concerns itself mostly with boating matters such as registration and safe boating.

NSW Fisheries
17 Shirley Road, Wollstonecraft, NSW 2065. Phone: 9438 5046.

Call Fisheries to find out about legal limits, permitted gear, spearfishing, areas where nets may not be used and so forth. No permit is required for recreational fishing. Fisheries publishes the Sydney Harbour Fishing Guide which anyone wanting to fish in the harbour should have, if only to be sure of exclusion zones.

There are two main zones on Sydney Harbour where fishing or collecting is prohibited. Fishing is prohibited in the North Harbour Aquatic Reserve, which covers the waters of North Harbour south of a line drawn between Forty Baskets Beach, Balgowlah, and Manly Point and Little Manly Point, Manly; collecting is prohibited along the entire foreshore of Sydney Harbour. No seashore animals in this intertidal zone along the shore may be killed or collected. These include crabs, snails, worms, octopus, sea urchins, anemones, pipis, cockles, mussels, oysters and yabbies. Do not use these creatures for bait. Bait must be bought in a shop.

Waterways Authority (Fishing Office)
James Craig Road, Rozelle Bay, Rozelle 2039. Phone: 9555 2042. Waterways InfoLine: 13 12 56. Also, a recorded 24-hour service provides boating information, phone: 13 12 36.

Waterways should be informed of the presence of any interstate or foreign boat on the harbour, although registration requirements may be waived. Waterways publishes the Safe Boating Handbook which stipulates all requirements for boats on the harbour, including the formal requirements regarding how registration numbers may be displayed on boats. Any visitor hiring or launching a boat must have this handbook, which also outlines rules for avoiding collisions, reporting accidents etc.

FISHING TOURS

A number of fishing charter companies offer fishing tours on the harbour. The usual boast is that if the fish are there, you will catch them. Many of them are listed under Fishing in the Sydney Yellow Pages telephone directory. Some of the more established companies include:

Charter Boat Lormar
Phone: 9361 2650.
Eastsail Daily departures. Access from New Beach Road, Rushcutters Bay. Phone: 9327 1166.
Fishabout Tours Killara.
Phone: 9498 7340.
Fishing Australia Tours
5 Green Street, Maroubra Junction.
Phone: 9344 5047.
Quayside Fishing Tours
Unit 5, 13 Parsons street, Rozelle.
Phone: 9555 2600.

HARBOUR ISLANDS

The following harbour islands are administered by the Sydney Harbour National Park. The Information Office is located at Cadmans Cottage, 110 George Street, The Rocks. Phone: 9247 5033.

Clarke Island
Located near Darling Point, this one-hectare island was used in colonial times by a Lieutenant Clarke to grow vegetables but he gave up the idea when pilfering got out of control. The island offers natural bushland, open space and, above all, peace and quiet. There is clean drinking water and a toilet.

Fort Denison
Not far from the Sydney Opera House, this tiny, fortified island is now a tourist attraction, with tours departing regularly from the Sydney Harbour National Park Information Office in The Rocks. Once a prison for the most recalcitrant convicts, it was known as 'Pinchgut'—possibly because of the poor rations that were served. From time to time, plans to turn the island into a restaurant or a boutique hotel are floated—an idea that would make the convicts turn in their graves.

Goat Island
Near East Balmain, this substantial body of land has served as the site for a powder magazine (a place for the storage of gunpowder) and has housed an experimental medical rearch centre for the study of the bubonic plague. Convicts also lived and worked here. The island later housed a major shipyard and among the proposals to develop the place for tourist use is one that would restore the shipyard to commercial operation.

Now part of the Sydney Harbour National Park, the island was used as a venue for the 1998 Biennale with one artist filling the now unoccupied harbourmaster's house with a sea of white balloons.

Heritage tours are conducted on Mondays, Fridays and Saturdays starting at 1 pm and ghost tours run on Wednesdays at 7 pm. Contact the National Parks and Wildlife Service for details. Phone: 9977 6522.

Rodd Island
This minute island, only half a hectare in area, is located near Birkenhead Point and is notable for its historic buildings. It can be hired out for functions.

Shark Island
This 1.5-hectare island off Rose Bay has seen many uses over the years, including animal quarantine. The island can be hired for functions and it offers grassy open space, a gazebo that can accommodate up to 30 people, rocky foreshores and sandy beaches. It has clean drinking water and toilets.

HIDEAWAYS

Bradleys Head Mosman, page 57.
Castle Rock Beach Balgowlah, page 35.
Cobblers Beach Middle Head, **Georges Heights**, page 45.
Collins Beach Manly, page 18.
Ewenton Park Balmain, page 111.
Fisher Bay Mosman, page 38.
Forty Baskets Beach Balgowlah, page 31.
Kellys Bush Reserve Woolwich, page 95.
Whiting Beach Mosman, page 59.
Lady Bay Beach South Head, **Watson's Bay**, page 148.
Lavender Bay North Sydney, page 75.
Manns Point Park Woolwich, page 82.
McKell Park Darling Point, page 138.

Obelisk Beach Middle Head, Georges Heights, page 46.
Peppercorn Park Drummoyne, page 98
Reef Beach Balgowlah, page 33.
Sawmiller Park McMahons Point, page 77.
Sydney Harbour National Park Balgowlah, page 32.
Taylors Bay beach Bradleys Head, page 56.
Washaway Beach Balgowlah, page 34.

RESTAURANTS AND CAFES (HARBOURSIDE)

Many clubs also have restaurants overlooking the harbour. This is a small selection only.

BIRKENHEAD POINT AND GLEBE

Cafe Birkenhead Shop 46, Birkenhead Point Centre. Access from Victoria Road, Drummoyne. Phone: 9181 4339.
Doyle's Bistro at the Markets Sydney Fish Market, Pyrmont Bridge Road, Pyrmont. Phone: 9552 4339.
Liners Cafe and Restaurant Birkenhead Point. Access from Victoria Road, Drummoyne. Phone: 9181 2527.
The Quarter Deck Restaurant Birkenhead Point. Access from Victoria Road, Drummoyne. Phone: 9181 2717.

DARLING HARBOUR

Jordon's Seafood Restaurant Access from Darling Drive, Sydney. Phone: 9281 3711.
Jo-Jo's Harbourside Restaurant Access from Darling Drive, Sydney. Phone: 9281 3888.

KIRRIBILLI AND McMAHONS POINT

Ensemble Theatre Restaurant 78 McDougall Street, Kirribilli. Phone: 9929 0644.
Sails Restaurant 2 Henry Lawson Avenue, McMahons Point. Phone: 9955 5793.

MANLY

Cove Seafood Restaurant Manly Wharf, The Esplanade, Manly. Phone: 9976 2400.
Manly Pier Restaurant Manly Wharf, The Esplanade, Manly. Phone: 9949 1994.

Romans on Pier Manly Wharf, The Esplanade, Manly. Phone: 9977 8877.

MOSMAN

Orso The Spit. Phone: 9968 3555.
Fresh Ketch Parriwi Road, The Spit. Phone: 9969 5665.
Harry's Fish Cafe 235 Military Road. The Spit. Phone: 9968 3049.
Shores Restaurant of Middle Harbour. Parriwi Road, The Spit. Phone: 9960 3391.
Spitlers The Spit. Phone: 9968 3811.
The Bathers Pavilion Restaurant Access from The Esplanade, Balmoral Beach, Balmoral. Phone: 9968 1133.
The Watermark Restaurant Access from The Esplanade, Balmoral Beach, Balmoral. Phone: 9968 3433.

ROSE BAY

Catalina Lyne Park, off New South Head Road, Rose Bay. Phone: 9371 0555.
Imperial Peking Afloat Lyne Park, off New South Head Road, Rose Bay. Phone: 9371 7955.
Pier Restaurant 594 New South Head Road, Rose Bay. Phone: 9327 6561.

SYDNEY COVE

Bennelong Restaurant Sydney Opera House. Phone: 9250 7478.
Doyle's at the Quay Customs Officers Stairs. Phone: 9252 3400.
Harbour Restaurant Sydney Opera House. Phone: 9250 7191.
Imperial Chinese Restaurant Customs Officers Stairs. Phone: 9247 9850.
Imperial Harbourside Restaurant 15 Circular Quay, Sydney. Phone: 9247 7073.
Italian Village Restaurant Customs Officers Stairs. Phone: 9247 6111.
Park Hyatt Hotel Restaurant, The Verandah 7 Hickson Road, The Rocks. Phone: 9241 1234.

QUAY

Quay Overseas Passenger Terminal. Phone: 9251 5600.
Sydney Oyster Bar Circular Quay East. Phone: 9247 2937
Waterfront Restaurant 27 Circular Quay West. Phone: 9247 3666.
Wolfie's Customs Officers Stairs. Phone: 9241 5577.

WALSH BAY

Harbourside Brasserie Pier One, Hickson Road, Dawes Point.

Phone: 9252 3000.
The Harbour Watch Seafood Restaurant Pier One, Hickson Road, Dawes Point. Phone: 9241 2217.
The Wharf Restaurant Pier 4, Hickson Road, Dawes Point. Phone: 9250 1761.
Watersedge Restaurant Pier One, Hickson Road, Dawes Point. Phone: 9247 4927.

WATSONS BAY

Doyle's on the Beach
11 Marine Parade, Watsons Bay. Phone: 9337 2007.
Doyle's Watsons Bay Hotel
10 Marine Parade, Watsons Bay. Phone: 9337 4299.

WOOLLOOMOOLOO BAY

Harry's Cafe de Wheels Cowper Wharf Roadway, Woolloomooloo. Phone: 9357 3074.

VAUCLUSE

Nielsen Park Kiosk Shark (Nielsen Park) Beach, Shark Bay, Vaucluse. Phone: 9337 1574.

SWIMMING POOLS

Including Harbour Baths and Enclosures

After heavy rain, some beaches and saltwater swimming pools, especially harbour baths, are closed because of pollution from stormwater drains. Telephone the relevant council for information, see page 158.

NORTHERN HARBOUR

NORTH HEAD TO MANLY

No pools.

MANLY TO SPIT BRIDGE

Clontarf Park beach Clontarf, page 36.
Fairlight Beach Fairlight, page 28.
Forty Baskets Beach Balgowlah, page 31.

SPIT BRIDGE TO SYDNEY HARBOUR BRIDGE

Balmoral Beach Mosman, page 44.
Clifton Gardens Reserve Clifton Gardens, page 55.
MacCallum Pool Shell Cove Park,

Cremorne. Phone: 9978 4000. See page 63.

SYDNEY HARBOUR BRIDGE TO IRON COVE BRIDGE

Greenwich Pool O'Connell Street, Greenwich. Entrance fee. Phone: 9438 5922. See page 84.
North Sydney Olympic Pool Milsons Point. Entrance fee. Phone: 9955 2309. See page 74.

SOUTHERN HARBOUR

IRON COVE BRIDGE TO SYDNEY OPERA HOUSE

Dawn Fraser Pool Elkington Park, Balmain. Entrance fee. Phone: 9555 1903. See page 104.

SYDNEY OPERA HOUSE TO SOUTH HEAD

Andrew (Boy) Charlton Pool Mrs Macquaries Road, The Domain. Entrance fee. Phone: 9358 6686. See page135.
Parsley Bay Vaucluse, page 145.
Redleaf Pool Double Bay. Phone: 9328 2018. See page 140.
Shark (Nielsen Park) Beach Nielsen Park, Vaucluse, page 143.
Watsons Bay baths Watsons Bay, page 146.

TOURS AND MUSEUMS

Balmain Historic Tour starts at Thornton Park, Balmain. For more details contact Leichhardt Council Library. Phone: 9367 9266.

Bradleys Head, Mosman The National Parks and Wildlife Service runs a nocturnal animals night tour. Phone: 9977 6522.

Fort Denison off Mrs Macquaries Point, Sydney. The National Parks and Wildlife Service runs regular tours to the island. Phone: 9977 6522.

Garden Island Naval Base between Wolloomooloo Bay and Elizabeth Bay. The Royal Australian Navy conducts tours of the base, which is Australia's largest as well as being full of history. The RAN also operates museums at Garden Island and at Spectacle Island near Birkenhead Point. Phone the Naval Historian's Office: 9359 2371.

Goat Island near Balmain. Heritage tours are conducted on Mondays, Fridays and Saturdays starting at 1 pm and ghost tours run once a

week on Wednesdays at 7 pm.
A Water Rats tour also runs regularly. Contact the National Parks and Wildlife Service for details. Phone: 9977 6522.

Government House Royal Botanic Gardens, Sydney. Free tours of this historic house, traditionally the home of the Governor of New South Wales, are conducted on Fridays, Saturdays and Sundays at 10.30 am.

Greycliffe House a historic Wentworth family home in Nielsen Park, is open weekdays from 9 am to 5 pm. Phone: 9337 5511.

Middle Head fortifications
Georges Heights. Tours are run by the National Parks and Wildlife Service. Phone: 9977 6522.

"Nutcote" 5 Walkaringa Avenue, Neutral Bay. This museum and shop was the harbourside home of noted children's author and illustrator May Gibbs. Phone: 9953 4453.

Old Quarantine Station North Head, Manly. Contact the National Parks and Wildlife Service for information on the various day and night tours available. Phone: 9977 6522. See page 17.

Taronga Zoo Mosman, has daily tours, including daybreak breakfast tours. Phone: 9969 2777. See page 58.

Sydney Harbour Bridge Climb
Tours to the top of the bridge. Phone: 9252 0077.

Sydney Opera House Bennelong Point, Sydney. Tours run regularly. Phone: 9250 7111.

Vaucluse House Vaucluse Bay, Vaucluse. Open daily for tours. Phone: 9388 7922.

USEFUL ADDRESSES

Clean Up Australia Campaign
Ian Kiernan
117 Harris Street, Pyrmont, NSW 2007. Phone: 9552 6177

Darling Harbour Authority
Level 6, 2 Market Street, Darling Harbour, NSW 2000.
Phone: 9286 0111.

National Parks and Wildlife Service
(Sydney Harbour National Park)
43 Bridge Street, Hurstville, NSW 2220. Phone: 9585 6444 (head office).

New South Wales Fisheries
12 Shirley Road, Wollstonecraft, NSW 2065. Phone: 9438 5046. Information Line: 9566 7802.

New South Wales Water Police
Wharf 25, Harris Street, Pyrmont, NSW 2009. Phone: 9692 5411.

Office of Marine Administration
PO Box 11, Millers Point, NSW 2001. Phone: 9364 2111.

Royal Botanic Gardens Visitor Centre
Mrs Macquaries Road, Sydney, NSW 2000. Phone: 9231 8125.

Sydney Organising Committee for the Olympic Games (SOCOG).
207 Kent Street, Sydney, NSW 2000. Phone: 9297 2000.

Sydney Ports Corporation
PO Box 25, Millers Point, NSW 2000. Phone: 9296 4999

Sydney Visitors Centre
106 George Street, The Rocks, NSW 2000. (Open 7 days). Phone: 9255 1788.

Tourism New South Wales
Level 2, 55 Harrington Street, The Rocks, NSW 2000. Phone: 9931 1111.

Waterways Authority
207 Kent Street, Sydney, NSW, 2001. Phone: 9563 8511 (head office). Waterways Infoline: 13 12 56. Recorded Information (24 hours): 13 12 36.

WALKS

NORTHERN HARBOUR

Sydney Harbour National Park–North Head–Manly
Starting either at Collins Beach, Little Manly, or at the former St Patrick's Seminary, North Head, this walk could exceed three kilometres if you decided to walk south from St Patrick's along the coastal edge of the park, west as far as Collins Beach and then a few hundred metres farther to Little Manly Point Park. Conditions are rough at the northern end but the paths start getting easier from the carpark at North Head onwards. This is not a walk for the unfit, although most of it is not

unduly hilly. A bracing and exciting walk, it has marvellous views out to sea and up the harbour to the city skyline. No refreshments are available en route. There are some signs.

Manly–The Spit

This is probably the best walk on the harbour and it is certainly the longest, stretching for approximately six-and-a-half kilometres. It winds along the edges of Manly Cove, Sydney Harbour, North Harbour and Middle Harbour through rugged bushland and patches of rainforest, along beaches and across parks and reserves. The only refreshments en route are available at the kiosk at Clontarf, so you will need to take water for this long walk.

While the walk in general is not difficult—a moderate level of fitness is required—at times the climbs are steep and rough, so don't forget to wear appropriate boots. The rewards for your effort are marvellous—hideaway beaches, sweeping harbour views and Aboriginal middens (remnants of past feasts). Historic plaques detail such events as the spearing of Captain Phillip at Collins Beach. There is a forest of beautiful red gums, clinging to rocks. Some of the country looks as it must have when Captain Arthur Phillip first sailed into the harbour in 1788. Only once or twice the track ducks onto roads. Blue signposts mark the way. *Highly recommended*.

Edwards Beach–Balmoral Beach–Georges Head

This pleasant walk runs a little over one kilometre, mostly on pathways, from Edwards Beach in the north, past Rocky Point and along Balmoral Beach to Georges Head. This walk is suitable for the moderately unfit—it is really more of a long stroll. There is much to see—the beach, the view over Middle Harbour, the restaurants, other walkers, and picnickers, many of whom descend upon the adjacent park in enormous groups on sunny weekends. There are plenty of shops across the road, too.

Sydney Harbour National Park–Middle Head, Georges Heights

This walk starts at the carpark next to the Naval Base at the end of Middle Head Road. One route takes you down to the southern shore of Middle Head via a gentle bush path to Obelisk, a nude beach that is generally regarded as a gay beach. The other goes to Cobblers, another nude, mainly gay, beach on the northern shore of Middle Head. It is accessed via a steep and difficult climb—only for the reasonably fit. There are no refreshments available en route and neither the walk nor the climb exceed one kilometre. There are no signs.

Clifton Gardens Reserve–Bradleys Head–Taronga Zoo–Little Sirius Cove
This superb walk takes you through mostly bush country but on quite well-made tracks with few steep slopes—more than three kilometres in all and never a dull moment. A reasonably fit person should have no problem. Starting at Clifton Gardens Reserve, Clifton Gardens, walk south through bush to Bradleys Head, not forgetting to climb down to the delightful hideaway beach at Taylors Bay on the way. Then walk around historic Bradleys Head and on to Taronga Zoo Wharf. From here you can visit the zoo, catch a ferry to Circular Quay or take another bush track west past Whiting Beach and along the zoo wall to end up at Little Sirius Cove Park. There are some signs.

Mosman Bay–Cremorne Point–Shell Cove
This walk can be commenced at one of three starting points: Reid Park (at the top of Mosman Bay off The Avenue, Mosman), Shell Cove Beach (at the top of Shell Cove, off Shell Cove Road, Neutral Bay) or the ferry wharf at Cremorne Point. The walk winds through unspoilt bushland—on one side is luxury housing, on the other is the water. Follow well-signposted well-made sealed paths past MacCallum Pool, Cremorne Wharf, Old Cremorne Wharf and the Mosman Rowers Club. At about two-and-a-half kilometres and with few steep slopes, this walk is suitable for moderately fit people. Refreshments are available en route, on the Mosman Bay side.

Mary Booth Park–Bradfield Park–Lavender Bay
This walk starts at Mary Booth Park (off Kirribilli Avenue, Kirribilli) and is signposted. Head west along the water's edge and enjoy the magnificent views across Port Jackson to the city skyline. Passing Jeffrey Street Wharf, walk under the Sydney Harbour Bridge—a wonderful sight—across Bradfield Park and, passing North Sydney Olympic Pool, continue along a boardwalk around the old Luna Park site, sadly now closed, into Lavender Bay. Here you find another attractive park (Quiberie), newly developed. Continue west around the bay and you will eventually end up at a beautiful hillside park—too steep for unfit people—called Watt Park. It is crossed by a piece of industrial history in the form of an

elevated railway line, beside which, in Harbour View Crescent, you will see the house formerly occupied by the famous painter, Brett Whiteley. Refreshments can be purchased en route at the pool kiosk.

Balls Head Reserve

This magnificent elevated bushland park is ringed by a one-and-a-half-kilometre walking track with superb views. The walk has an added advantage in that, being circular, you are never far from the centrally located carpark should you get tired. With lovely views, peaceful bush, few slopes and some nice places to rest along the way, who could ask for more? Refreshments are not available but there are some great picnic areas with all facilities.

Gore Cove–Berry Island Reserve

A little under two kilometres in all, this harbourside walk through occasional dense bush is undulating with plenty of small slopes, some tree roots to step over and plenty of twists and turns—the sort of walk that is good for flexibility. Moderately fit people should have no problems. Start either from Holloway Park beside the western shore of Gore Cove (off Vista Street, Greenwich) or from Berry Island Reserve (off Shirley Road, Wollstonecraft). The views are spectacular from the elevated harbour end of Berry Island, a former island now linked to land by a grassy open park. While the walking is pretty here, there are not many picnic or resting points—except close to Shirley Road—and no refreshments are available en route. Still, because it is so wild in parts, it does have the feeling of an adventure walk. There is parking in the street.

Bond Reserve–Manns Point

Starting at the pretty little park beside the Greenwich Sailing Club called Bonds Reserve (off Prospect Street, Greenwich) walk east along a nice track through light bush to Manns Point Reserve. This walk has both seashore and elevated sections beside the Shell oil terminal. Both parks are small and the walk is short—about half a kilometre—with a hill at the Manns Point end. It is a nice stroll to Manns Point, even with picnic basket in hand, and the view across the harbour from the point itself justifies the modest effort. No refreshments are available en route.

Greenwich Wharf–Shell Park

Arriving either by ferry or by car, it is best to start this walk at Greenwich Wharf, at the end of Greenwich Point Road. The walk then proceeds north along the shore of the

Parramatta River, terminating in the delightful elevated Shell Park, with its fine grassy areas and tennis courts. The park has plenty of nice spots to rest or look at the view. The vegetation is parkland rather than bushland, with houses alongside. A pleasant and refreshing spot, it is well worth a visit. The walk is about one kilometre long, mostly flat with a few gentle slopes. No refreshments are available en route and parking is scarce.

Woolwich Lookout–Clarkes Point
Woolwich Lookout on Woolwich Road, while not strictly harbourside, is high and has magnificent views. It links directly to harbourside parkland, (some of which is still in dispute between citizens' groups and developers), including Clarkes Point Park. This park of open bushland, spacious grassy areas and pleasant water views is one of the best on the harbour. It also has barbecue facilities and toilets. The walk to the park from the lookout is not so much linear as rambling. It involves some steep slopes, but is not long—600 to 750 metres, depending on which route you take—and the facilities at Clarkes Point justify a little effort. No refreshments can be bought en route but there is a convenient pub at Woolwich Lookout.

Southern Harbour

Bicentennial, Jubilee and Federal parks, Glebe
This is not a linear walk but a large, open, rambling place. Recently developed, and certainly with no bushland in sight, it allows you to make your own route over its pleasant and mostly flat areas.
A short walk of about 600 to 750 metres, perhaps more, can be constructed, with lots of views of the 'working harbour', the Glebe Island Bridge and the city skyline. There are plenty of pleasant spots to have a picnic and refreshments are available along Glebe Point Road.

Darling Harbour
This is not so much a walk as an extended stroll and, far from being bushland, the scenery is intensely urban. However, this development is an excellent example of urban redevelopment, a splendidly planned and executed remake of what was once derelict waterside industrial land. There is plenty to see, lots of refreshments available, and remarkable close-up views of the city skyline. One possible way of exploring the area is to start from the Sydney Aquarium on the eastern side of the bay near the Pyrmont Bridge walkway and to walk south past the

IMAX giant screen cinema and Tumbalong Park to the Chinese Gardens opposite the Exhibition Centre. Turning north, make your way past the shopping complex on the western side of the bay to the Australian National Maritime Museum. The whole area is totally flat and this suggested walk is about two kilometres long.

Sydney Cove
This easy, flat walk—beginning at the Hyatt Hotel on the water at western Circular Quay—offers unforgettable views and intense urban sophistication with plenty of places to purchase refreshments en route. The walk goes past the restaurant quarter at Customs Officers Steps, the Museum of Contemporary Art, the Circular Quay ferry terminals (from which ferries leave for all parts of the harbour) and then continues on to the Sydney Opera House precinct. At the Botanic Gardens Gate on the eastern side of the Opera house it joins up with another walk around Farm Cove so don't forget to wear your comfortable walking shoes.

Farm Cove–Mrs Macquaries Chair
This walk returns to the parkland that characterises most harbourside walks. It passes through the Royal Botanic Gardens on Farm Cove—so named because it was the site of the first farm in the new colony—before arriving at the splendid viewing area at Mrs Macquaries Chair. This point offers spectacular views of the city skyline, the Sydney Opera House, the Sydney Harbour Bridge and Fort Denison as well as sweeping views of the Lower North Shore and right down the harbour toward the heads. There is often a person selling soft drinks here. Continue south from Mrs Macquaries Chair, following the eastern side of Woolloomooloo Bay, past the Andrew (Boy) Charlton Swimming Pool to Woolloomooloo, a harbourside suburb noted for its working-class history, pubs and cafes. Or make your way up the slight hill to the Art Gallery of New South Wales, overlooking the bay. The total distance is about one kilometre and the way is mostly flat and paved.

Rose Bay–Lyne Park
Commence this walk from the western end of the bay at Point Piper. Flat, paved footpaths run along the edge of Rose Bay itself, past the ferry wharf and through or around Lyne Park. The park is a pleasant, open area beside the water, and you might be lucky enough to catch sight of a seaplane landing near the jetty. An RSL Club and several restaurants

in the area offer a range of eating options. The distance is about one kilometre and the stroll is not taxing.

The Hermitage–Nielsen Park

This highly enjoyable Eastern Suburbs walk begins either at Rose Bay Convent—a school off New South Head Road—or from the western end of Nielsen Park. The walk, which is less than two kilometres long, requires a moderate degree of fitness and offers magnificent glimpses of the harbour right down to the bridge and the city skyline.

The track is rough and uneven and has quite a few steps, but the dense bush, birdlife and the isolation to be found at lovely Queens, Hermit Bay and Milk beaches makes the effort worthwhile. Nielsen Park itself has terrific elevated views over the harbour. No refreshments are available en route, but Nielsen Park Kiosk has a small take-away cafe as well as a first-class restaurant.

Parking is meagre anywhere along the route but you can arrive by bus at either end.

Watsons Bay–Camp Cove–South Head

Watsons Bay can be reached by car (although parking is difficult, especially on weekends), or by bus or ferry from Circular Quay. Starting at the ferry wharf, walk north along the waterfront, past the Doyle's Watsons Bay Hotel and famous Doyle's on the Beach seafood restaurant (there are plenty of refreshments available on this walk up to Camp Cove). Winding briefly through the streets of cottages behind Camp Cove, you will soon arrive at Camp Cove beach, a fashionable Eastern Suburbs meeting place for generations of people. Walk along the beach itself then climb the steps at the northern end of the beach into Sydney Harbour National Park. Here, a well-made path leads toward South Head, and soon offers unsurpassed views right up the harbour to the city, then across to Manly and, as you round the point, out to sea. Drink in the clean wind rising off the Pacific Ocean—an exhilarating moment. Along the way, you will pass Lady Bay Beach, a nude beach, which can be accessed by climbing down a steep track. This walk is nearly three kilometres.

Further Reading

Drumm, Ken (1992) *Spectacular Sydney*, Ken Drumm, Sydney.

Great Outdoors Publications (1998) *Great Outdoors Tide Guide*, Great Outdoors Publications, Sydney.

Gunter, John (1995) *Sydney by Ferry and Foot* (4th edition), Kangaroo Press, Sydney.

Matthews, Phillip (1997) *The Waterways of Sydney Harbour*, Phillip Matthews Book Publishers, Sydney.

Moore, Wendy (1996) *This Is Sydney*, New Holland Publishers Pty Ltd, Sydney.

Moore, Wendy (1998) *Sydney In A Week* (revised edition), New Holland Publishers Pty Ltd, Sydney.

Park, Margaret [editor] (1997) *Doors Were Always Open*, City West Development Corporation, Sydney.

Rose, John [originating editor] (1998) *The New South Wales Fishing Atlas*, Penguin Books, Melbourne.

Shore, Harvey (1995) *From The Quay*, UNSW Press, Sydney.

Smith, Vivian & Grey, Robert (eds) (1992) *Sydney's Poems*, Primavera Press, Sydney.

Sydney Convention Centre (1997) *Member Services Directory*, Sydney Convention Centre, Sydney.

Waterways Authority (1997) *Safe Boating Handbook*, Waterways Authority, Sydney.

Index